CHRISTOS TSIOLKAS

Christos Tsiolkas was born in Melbourne in 1965. His novel, *Loaded*, was published in 1995 (adapted for the screen as *Head On*, 1998) and his second novel, *The Jesus Man*, was published in 1999. He is the co-author of *Jump Cuts: An Autobiography*, a dialogue written with Sasha Soldatow. Christos' plays include *Who's Afraid of the Working Class?*, *Viewing Blue Poles*, *Elektra AD*, *Dead Caucasians* and *Fever*. Along with Spiro Economopoulos, he co-wrote and co-directed the short film, *Thug*, for SBS Television. Christos has also worked as a reviewer, essayist and journalist.

He is currently working on a new novel, *Dead Europe*, the screenplay for *Who's Afraid of the Working Class?*, as well as working with Spiro Economopoulos on a play titled *Non Parlo di Salo* about the political and artistic legacy of filmmaker Pier Paolo Pasolini. Christos lives in Melbourne with his lover Wayne van der Stelt.

the devil's playground

CHRISTOS TSIOLKAS

CURRENCY PRESS, SYDNEY

SCREENSOUND AUSTRALIA
NATIONAL SCREEN AND SOUND ARCHIVE

First published by Currency Press Pty Ltd and ScreenSound Australia in 2002

Currency Press Pty Ltd
PO Box 2287, Strawberry Hills
NSW 2012 Australia
enquiries@currency.com.au
www.currency.com.au

ScreenSound Australia
National Screen and Sound Archive
GPO Box 2002, Canberra
ACT 2601 Australia
enquiries@screensound.gov.au
www.screensound.gov.au

Australian Screen Classics series: ISSN 1447-557X

National Library of Australia—Cataloguing-in-Publication Data:
    Tsiolkas, Christos, 1965– .
    The devil's playground.
    Bibliography.
    ISBN 0 86819 671 1.
    1. The devil's playground (Motion picture). 2. Feature films—Australia—History and criticism. 3. Motion pictures, Australian. 4. Seminarians—Victoria—Drama. I. Title. (Series: Australian screen classics series).
    791.4372

Cover design by Kate Florance, Currency Press; see the list of illustrations. The images in this book are from the ScreenSound Australia collection: copyright © Fred Schepisi.
Typeset by Currency Press in Iowan Old Style roman 9.5 pt.
Printed by Southwood Press.

The Series Editor wishes to thank David McKnight for his political expertise, and the Department of Art History and Theory at the University of Sydney and the Australian Film, Television and Radio School for their generous support.

For Spiro Economomopoulos, who keeps me excited and challenged about film, and for Wayne van der Stelt, who makes all of this possible.

AUSTRALIAN SCREEN CLASSICS

JANE MILLS
Series Editor

Our national cinema plays a vital role in our cultural heritage and in showing us what it is to be Australian. But the picture can be blurred by unruly forces including competing artistic aims, inconstant personal tastes, political vagaries, constantly changing priorities in screen education and training, and technological innovations and market forces.

When these forces remain unconnected, the result can be an artistically impoverished cinema and audiences who are disinclined to seek out and derive pleasure from a diverse range of films.

Screen culture, of which this series is a part, is the glue needed to stick these forces together. It's the plankton in the food chain that feeds the imagination of our filmmakers and their audiences. It's what makes sense of the opinions, memories, responses, knowledge and exchange of ideas about film.

Above all, screen culture is informed by a *love* of cinema. And it has to be carefully nurtured if we are to understand and appreciate the aesthetic, moral, intellectual and sentient value of our national cinema.

Australian Screen Classics will match some of our best-loved films with some of our most distinguished writers and thinkers, drawn from the worlds of culture, criticism and politics. All we ask of our writers is that they feel passionate about the films they choose. Through these thoughtful, elegantly-written books, we hope that screen culture will work its sticky magic.

CONTENTS

LIST OF ILLUSTRATIONS

'Your body is your worst enemy': Brother Francine (Arthur Dignam) in the pool shower room.

I

An Antipodean summer merges one year into another, and similarly, my memories of the summers of the late 1970s merge together. I begin thus because I have to admit that I cannot recall the exact date that I first saw *The Devil's Playground*. It must have been a summer's weekend because I remember a hot blast of sun hitting my face as I stumbled out of the theatre in Melbourne, and I furiously scrubbed at my cheeks to remove the telltale signs of the tears I had cried. Other things I remember of that summer in which 1977 merged into 1978 include sitting on a chair at the barbers and flicking guiltily through a cheap soft-porn magazine— the sort that combined lurid photographs of big-breasted girls with sensationalist editorials on vice and sin. There were photographs of pale, angry British youths dressed in bin liners, safety pins through their clothes, and I recall thinking how frightening these young punks looked. I remember my voice breaking and I remember showing my friend Jane my first pubes.

The production notes for *The Devil's Playground* state that it was completed in 1976. By the end of the following year I was twelve and I am sure that I was at least that old before I saw the film. Maybe this is a conceit. I identified so strongly with Tom Allen, the film's central character, that I want to believe I was the exact same age as he: thirteen. Reminiscences always carry the danger of nostalgic reconstruction, but I do remember telling a teacher how I 'liked that film a lot' and she scrunched up her nose and asked me bluntly, 'Do your parents know the kind of films you're watching?'. An odd question.

My mother, who loved films and passed on this love to me, would come along with me to see *Coming Home* or *An Unmarried Woman* or *Alien*. She also took me to *Gone With the Wind* and *It Happened One Night* and, unbeknownst to her, handed down to me her passion for Clark Gable. Admittedly, trekking off to the cinema with my mother was somewhat embarrassing. The last thing a boy entering adolescence wants is to be seen hanging out with a parent. Nevertheless, the red cheeks were worth it. As she bought the tickets, I gained access to many films I wasn't meant to see. For her, she got a translator by her side.

'What did she say? What's going on now?'

Around us the old Australian women would purse their lips and occasionally give us a serve.

'Shut up. We're here to see a movie, not listen to you wogs shout.'

My mother would be incensed. I would sink lower and lower into my seat. It wasn't till years later, going to the movies in Athens, that I would realise how strange Australian movie going must have seemed to my parents. In Greece they do shout commandments and insults to the screen. As an adult I was to understand my mother's fierce, passionate interaction with the melodramas and themes unfolding on the screen as a means of communicating her love of film to me. But at thirteen, I was only conscious of her difference. I recoiled from her, from her 'wogginess'.

I started keeping certain movies from mum.

The Devil's Playground was one of these. I had seen the trailer. I do remember that clearly. I remember making a mental note to make sure that I saw the film. What I had responded to were the images of the boys in the shower, the craggy ocker profile of the actor Nick Tate, who plays Brother Victor in the film. If I had no words for these instinctual responses to the images— homosexuality was, if not unknown, certainly not a word I would dare attach to myself—they were strong enough to make me seek out the strange, the difficult and the esoteric.

The Devil's Playground was not a film any of my friends would have chosen to see. Just as I kept it from my mother, I also knew to go to the film alone, knew that there would be something dangerous in explaining my keen need to see it to any of my schoolyard friends. So sometime in the summer of 1977 and 1978, alone, in a nearly empty cinema, I saw the film.

Brother Victor smoking a cigarette. Tom Allen's smile and Tom Allen's arse. The underwater sirens attacking Brother Francine's naked body. Two boys giving each other a clumsy hand job in the dark. The reflection of the trees on the car window as Tom is driven towards Melbourne and away from the seminary. The nausea I felt when Brother Victor condemns the seminary rules as 'unnatural', as making 'poofters' of the boys. Tom hanging out his piss-wet sheets to dry and rubbing his hands together against the cold winter air.

Looking through this list of memories, it strikes me as odd that I have included nothing about faith and spirituality, nothing about God. Like Tom, the film's young protagonist, I too was determined to follow a Christian God into good works and self-sacrifice. Also like Tom, I too was clutching at a permanent erection. It must have been that this religious struggle was part of what I was responding to. I have no other explanation for why the tears flowed so strongly after seeing the film.

It also strikes me that I was responding to the beauty within the film. *The Devil's Playground* is full of sensual images. The film is all water and flesh—the fresh, smooth faces of the boys, the ragged, ageing profiles of the Brothers. The colours are cold but starkly intense—all blues and greens. In a sense, one of the reasons that the film has remained in my memory is that it is so ravishing to look at.

I have returned to *The Devil's Playground* time and time again and each return has made me bring new questions and perspectives to the film. But what I want to convey about that first viewing is what it meant for a young teenage boy to suddenly see what is possible in cinema. Beyond the narrative of adolescent confusion and spiritual alienation, I responded to the canvas of the moving image. Beginning with a slow, languid tracking shot up a river, the screen pulsating with young flesh falling and playing in the water, I was enchanted by the ability of cinema to astonish me, to recreate and, more importantly, to re-imagine my sensory world.

As spectacle, the cinema had entranced me from the beginning. What made the experience of watching *The Devil's Playground* different was the narrative of early adolescence that resonated completely with my own experiences and circumstances. This was an experience emotionally and viscerally different to watching the raid on the Death Star in *Star Wars*. The sense that movies were not only about entertainment, or about fantasy, was an electric charge for me at thirteen.

That summer of *The Devil's Playground* is also the summer when I stumbled into the small auditorium of an art house cinema and saw the Italian film, *Padre Padrone*. I believe that there are moments in life, rare but unquestionable, in which an experience transforms consciousness. My lifelong love of film can be traced back to my love of spectacle—but the imperative to make cinema central to my intellectual and emotional life can be traced back to that period of my youth in which I read myself in the confused, Catholic boyhood of Tom Allen and in the harsh, patriarchal servitude of the shepherd boy in *Padre Padrone*.

Of course, I was neither a Sardinian shepherd nor a Catholic schoolboy. But in a sense both these films spoke eloquently to the differing worlds I found myself in. The Mediterranean agrarian poverty of the Taviani brothers' film was the world from which my parents had emerged. School was becoming, for me, the place where my parent's world, concerns and values were excluded and where I strived to discover what it might mean to be Australian. I think it was this dislocation, trying to make sense of an old world—Greece—and a new promise—Australia—that partly led to the tears I shed. Whether it was God or home or even something called masculinity, I felt close to the innocent Tom, trying to be a good boy but betrayed always by my cock, my fantasies, my daydreams and my wish for freedom. Until I had the means and the capabilities for this freedom, the dark caverns of movie houses became its closest approximation.

In *Padre Padrone* the abused, illiterate shepherd boy eventually takes himself back to school, completes his education and writes the autobiographical book which will inspire the filmmakers. This yearning for an education, which also symbolised an avenue to independence and freedom, was what I wanted for myself. This particular yearning is not visible in *The Devil's Playground*, but I always imagined that the young Tom Allen was to grow up and become the director Fred Schepisi. Tom's inability to remain faithful to the Bible's vengeful God is truly a pagan celebration of the body and the senses, as Pauline Kael so deftly pointed out in her review of the film.[1] But if his instinctual pursuit for freedom is not distilled in a thirst for knowledge or enlightenment, there is nevertheless a strong sense of this particular film being Schepisi's *Portrait of the Artist as a Young Man*. It may say more about the 'Australianness' of this film that an intellectual direction for Tom is so adroitly avoided. No-one suggests to him—neither teachers nor family—that possibly the crafts of the imagination are the natural home for such an inquisitive, passionate and restless boy.

It is only in retrospect that it strikes me as astonishing that I was barely an adolescent and that I had sat through *The Devil's Playground* and *Padre Padrone*. And sitting through is far too inadequate a description. I was entranced, knocked out, stupefied—and yet it would be a rewriting of personal history to not admit that for periods I was also bored and confused. This was a language no-one had assumed a need to teach me. If I could not make complete sense of the films I had viewed, it did not matter as much as the fact that I had glimpsed possibilities and freedom.

I don't think that freedom is too strong a word. At the end of *The Devil's Playground* Tom runs away from school and hitchhikes towards the big city. The shepherd's son in *Padre Padrone* gains his education and writes his book. If I had been born into a previous generation, or possibly, if I had been born into a different class, I may have found this sense of art's ability to liberate through literature. I had read enough already at thirteen to glimpse—just glimpse—that the nineteenth-century European world was full of precocious rich brats able to spout their philosophical epistles in Latin, classical Greek and French. But I had only my rudimentary demotic Greek, my prole Australian English and the world of the image. It was through deciphering and learning the language of image that I first gained the tools to re-imagine my world. Of course, I had to discover words, the richness of the written language, to make sense of these imaginings. Film became the bridge that allowed me to master the English language.

The critical heritage of popular music has a well-documented exploration of rock music as a means through which working-class lads found creative freedom and sometimes wealth and excess. There is cultural theorist Greil Marcus' deification of the white-trash Elvis; there is the class transcendence of British rock'n'roll and northern soul, a trajectory that takes us from the Beatles in 1960s Liverpool to the Happy Mondays and Oasis in post-acid house Manchester. The histories of jazz, soul, blues and hip-hop make little sense if their writers do not engage with the politics of race and the contradiction of class.

This is not a pronounced current in film criticism. The auteur theorists in the United States argued an aesthetics denuded of politics and the European critical tradition post-1968 became increasingly academic and elitist. The critical analysis by non-Western critics, for valid reasons, focused more on the effects and relationships of race and imperialism than on the subjectivities of working-class audiences. Even Marxist-derived film criticism has a very limited bibliography when it comes to the transformative experience of film watching and making for people from the working classes.

My viewing of films in itself did not place me outside the world I had been born to. My mother, my friends, in fact most of my social world watched and loved film. A process of alienation only began when the form of my cinema going began to change, when I started leaving behind the blockbuster and going to the foreign movie, when I sneaked into seeing something called *The Devil's Playground*.

Of course, there is a sense in which Tom Allen is forever etched in my mind as the young, fresh-faced child whose body refused repression. Water imagery suffuses *The Devil's Playground*, and Tom's adolescent body can't stop spurting. He pisses in his bed, he wanks and ejaculates. One reason why the film made such a strong impression on me, but did not shock or upset me, was that Tom's inability to command his body to be 'good'—in the narrow sense of his Catholic faith—did not condemn him to the tyranny of evil, to God's eternal silence. A couple of years after *The Devil's Playground* I was to see Ingmar Bergman's *The Seventh Seal*, and there I did experience true spiritual terror.[2] Schepisi vanquished the fears that the Brothers of Tom's faith had attempted to instil in him. Tom's very pagan body, his refusal to cleave his flesh into the opposites of 'good' and 'evil', came to me as a reprieve at thirteen. By allowing me a glimpse into a future not dominated by authoritarian or ascetic or tyrannical morality, it is no surprise that I left the cinema high, exhilarated and inspired. And it was no wonder that in Tom Allen I had finally encountered a hero—not the hero of the Western or science fiction, but a hero that seemed more flesh and blood than even the schoolmates around me.

In later years, going to the film again, I was to become aware that in its treatment of the adult characters—the celibate Brothers—the film was much less benign. But as a teenager, they were not of much concern to me.

I am thirteen and my perspective is that of the boys. Like them I am unaware of time, of the accumulated anguish of repression.

Also, like them, I am unaware that my very body itself is a tease, a challenge. I am too confused by the changes in my body to comprehend that it could be in any way desirable. My pubes are still flimsy and wiry, not yet bushy. My voice has not yet broken. I am having my first wet dreams. I am thirteen. I believe in the one true God of righteous justice and I believe in His Son, the Redeemer. I believe in Hell and I'm scared that I'm going to go there. It is a summer's day. I'm slipping into a theatre to see a movie that I sense I am not meant to see. I take a seat five rows from the front. The lights go down. The theatre is near empty. The movie, *The Devil's Playground*, begins.

1978

Your body is your worst enemy. Brother Francine

Across the road of my primary school—a state institution filled with the children of first generation immigrant Greeks, Italians, Turks and Slavs—was a small Catholic Church with a primary school attached. Though literally across the street, spitting distance, we rarely had any contact

Adolescent confessions: Tom (Simon Burke) and Waite (Alan Cinis) talk nervously in the woodshed.

with the kids who went there. They wore uniforms, which we didn't, and I remember asking my father if they were in training to be nuns and monks. He must have laughed; he probably told me a scatological, very funny anecdote involving monks, perversion and genitalia. My family was religious but blessedly sceptical of clerics.

I think it is necessary to preface an understanding of how I came to *The Devil's Playground* by stating that I was raised Greek Orthodox in a country whose colonial history was lacerated by divisions between Catholics and Protestants. It took me a long time to understand the ramifications of this history. I was raised understanding myself as divided from a British and Celtic majority, and I was raised in an environment of left political affiliation. The colonial history of the country, however, was formed through the conflicts, class antagonisms and divisions between Catholics (largely Celtic), the Protestants and Aboriginal Australians.

Later, as I grew into an awkward, literate adolescence, I was to become aware of how the conflicts between Micks and Proddies affected every aspect of political life in Australia. Frank Hardy's novel, *Power Without Glory*, a *roman à clef* detailing the machinations of Catholic power struggles, was set in the suburbs in which I grew up.[3] But all this was invisible to me in childhood.

Australian history was taught to us through the study of faceless human beings and no attempt was made to connect the past to our present and future. The story of Ned Kelly was told to us as history as well as legend, but again, its context remained unclear for us immigrant kids. Our parents would explain that because Australians were a 'nation of convicts', they made heroes out of their crooks. Kelly's Irishness, his Catholicism, all this remained silent. Sure, there was occasional violence, when insults were traded from either side of the school fences, and we'd set off to beat up the Catholic boys across the road. But for us immigrant kids the teasing had to do with nuns teaching them, the insults to do with their wearing of uniforms, and if we started fights, it was not because they were Micks but because they went to a private school.

We thought they were rich and spoilt. They weren't: these dark, greaso kids in their blue and grey uniform, in their red brick school with one tiny basketball court, across the road from the factories in which our mothers worked. That we thought they were speaks volumes for how ignorant we were. This was not an ignorance of class but of wealth itself: of privilege, and power and money. In my thirteenth year, Tom Allen's year, my mum and dad decided to move us further out, into the middle-class eastern suburbs of Melbourne. My new high school was now filled with Renees and Micks, Craigs and Brendas. From being one of a number of young boys with olive complexions and precocious pubic hair, I was now a 'darkie' amongst a sea of blondes and redheads. These redheads and blondes also had parents who worked in the same factories as did my own folk (though a significant proportion had mothers 'at home', fathers who were 'clerks'), but the unforced multi-ethnic camaraderie of my early years had gone. It makes perfect sense that it wasn't wealth that seemed the definitive marker of difference but the colour of skin, the slant of an eye, the accent of your English.

It was possibly a good thing that I first saw *The Devil's Playground* while I was still largely ignorant of how wealth functioned in society. When I saw the film again in my early twenties I felt a betrayal, only momentarily, but it felt like an assault on my memory of the innocence of it. Nothing in the script indicates

Tom's class background. But the genteel attentiveness of his mother and the imposing architecture of the collegiate grounds can't come cheap.

Till my early teens my experience was safe, limited to the wog working-class world of the inner city, populated by immigrants: a world in which loyalty to the Labor Party (the representative of the working class) was unwavering; a world in which I was looked after by a slew of tough, gentle women, who all worked with my mother; a world of good friends, Spanish and Yugoslav, Italian and Turkish, whose bodies looked like mine, smelt like mine. This experience was about to be fundamentally challenged by the move to a different school, a different part of town; challenged by my taking a short-lived but fundamental excursion into the orthodoxy of Baptist Christianity and away from the ritual, the ortho*praxy* of Eastern Orthodoxy. My past was itself being challenged by the very changes in my body, the strange disturbing violence of my desire. I make these observations because they are crucial to understanding my enrapture with the film. A few years' difference, a few years on, it's quite possible I would have detested it, that far from identifying with the film's young protagonist, his clear alabaster skin, his access to books and knowledge, all of this would have forced a separateness between himself and myself.

I don't know, I am running ahead of myself. There is much to say about the film and the country that produced it, much to say about the precariousness of criticism and aesthetic taste—but first there is the film.

I am in a movie theatre. Was it the Odeon on Burke Street? It is 1978.

The first thing I notice is the music. Bruce Smeaton's score is gentle, the simple piano chords immediately arresting. The second thing I notice are the titles. In a few years, when much of the film, its narrative, the order of the scenes, even some of the characters, will be forgotten, I will still remember the impact of the bold plates of pastel colours that sat on the giant screen. The actors' names were burnt in white over these vibrant blues and greens and reds. The music I was used to was the rousing, bombastic score of John Williams or Bill Conti.⁴ If I had seen beautiful titles before, or had listened to an elegant piece of film music, it would have been on the small screen of a black and white television, or the even smaller screen of our brand new colour television. I was used to movie actors speaking in tinkling mono.

Then the titles fade and a camera seems to be hovering and gliding through water. The screen is full of naked adolescent bodies. They jump and splash into a lake, they shiver on the banks, they pummel and dunk each other. The boys' bodies seem to shine white, an unearthly ghostly white. On the bank there is a man clothed fully in black, from neck to feet, obviously some kind of priest or religious man. His dark attire is in stark contrast to the near nakedness of the boys. An old priest, or as we are soon to find out, a Brother, is asleep on a bench. Behind him are the cold, imposing walls of the institution. The screen is filled with Simon Burke's face peering down into the camera. His torso is wet from the swim. There is nothing remotely sexual in the encounter between old man and young flesh, but the stark juxtaposition between bare flesh and dark cassock cloth is immediately disturbing. The young boy is Tom Allen, the thirteen-year-old protagonist of the movie. He runs across the schoolyard and is blocked by a fellow student. They tussle in a mock fight which ends with Tom on top of his mate, Waite (Alan Cinis). Waite asks him what he would like to do to him. Tom laughs and heaves himself off the other boy's body: 'Nothing'.

In the shower room, the boys are in separate cubicles. A tall, lean and deeply unhappy Brother—it is evident in his stern face—patrols the narrow lockers. He flings open the door to a cubicle and Tom is naked, showering, his fleshy buttocks white with soap. Brother Francine (Arthur Dignam) roars at him for bathing nude without his swimming suit and reminds him that, 'Your body is your worst enemy, Tom Allen'. The man proceeds to give the other boys a lecture on the purity of the soul, the curse of the body. He orders the boys to 'practice self-denial, self-examination, self-discipline' if they are to resist the temptations of Satan.

It is no wonder that the film resonated so strongly for me. Almost immediately it laid out the very conflicts that I was experiencing around emerging sexuality, a tortured religiosity and a changing, conflicted body. The film was obviously made for an adult audience. I was to understand it much later as a classic remembrance of childhood, but I did not perceive it as such at the time. I think the most telling aspect of this for me was that I was to forget completely the first title that was to appear over the graceful images: *Autumn, 1953*. It wasn't until revisiting the film as an adult that I was to realise that what I was watching was not a contemporaneous story. So fully was I prepared to identify with Tom Allen that I somehow allowed the historic referencing of the film to escape me, even in the very act of watching it for the first time.

Delicious: this describes something of the film experience, of watching the film that first time.

The most perceptive review I have read of the film, by Pauline Kael in the *New Yorker* (writing in 1981 when the film was eventually released in the United States), ends by praising Schepisi's ability to render the theological and sexual traumas of Catholicism in a benevolent, humane manner. She praises the director's 'humorous pagan eyes'. That would not have been my language at the time but I think it aptly conveys the film's matter-of-fact rendering of human sexuality. Tom remains a thoroughly likeable character throughout the film. His inability to stop wanking ('two or three times *a day*, Father'), to stop bed-wetting, to enable his will to mould his faith and conquer all the messy expulsions and secretions of his body, are not represented as failures but as a crucial victory for the natural expressions of his human body.

The images that remain from the film, images that have remained with me for a quarter of a century, all have to do with the intimate rendering of skin and texture: the texture of the cloth trousers into which Tom slides his hand in order to grab at his erection; the white nails on the two boys' fingers which scratch and pull at their skin as they sit in a woodshed, discussing penises and sex, their anxiety as intense as their delight.

Sex on the screen was not new for me. Everything from the tits and bums slapstick of the *Carry On* comedies to the counter-cultural successes of the Vietnam-era Hollywood cinema I had greedily watched, heavily edited, on our television. But I had very little to choose from in terms of an affirming depiction of sex and the body, between the camp dirty-mindedness in English films and the puritanical distaste for the body in most of American films. I am thinking here of *Klute, Midnight Cowboy, The Graduate, Carnal Knowledge*—which I had seen on TV, chopped and edited to buggery, to be sure, but which all made a huge impression on me for the challenge of their themes and depiction of taboo sex.

The rendering of flesh on the giant screen is one of the primal attractions of cinema. Instinctively we understand the pleasures of voyeurism and the eroticism of the moving celluloid image. This sensuality is not only about photographing flesh. If I think back to my initial responses to film, to becoming enamoured with film, I remember moments of swooning, truly orgasmic motion. They include a pan across a blighted, poor mining village in Ken Loach's *Kes*; the point of view of the shark as it speeds to gulp its victim in Steven Spielberg's *Jaws*; the swing of Aliki Vougiouklakis' hips in any number of my mother's favourite musicals. I was aware of the sensuality of cinema from an early age. What induced swooning while watching *The Devil's Playground*, I now understand, was the sensuality of its images and direction, the music, the performances, its damn sexiness with a narrative that naturalised masturbation and the hunger for sex. This sensuality saturated the film: the sounds and images of light and water were as erotic as the glimpses of skin and of flesh. Afterwards, as soon as the titles finished—and I stayed till the very end, till the house lights came up—I rushed to the cinema toilets, banged the bolt and came spraying come across the floor and door.

It was delicious. But it was also terrifying. The film may be pagan, to use Kael's term, in refusing monotheism's breach between body and soul, but it is nevertheless a movie deeply imbued with its own morality around the body and sex. If Tom's struggle is to escape the Catholic identification of flesh with sin, he's also faced with a further struggle: to see that there is only one appropriate sexual path, that of masculinity, straightness, a healthy sexuality that broaches neither perversion nor homosexuality.

Light infuses *The Devil's Playground*. The autumnal palette of the film perfectly captures the sombre but still vigorous colours of a Melbourne season. Even within the imposing architecture of the cathedral and school, light manages to play and dance its way through cracks, to gleam on surfaces. And the light that reflects on

Family bliss: Tom's family on a picnic.

the water of the lake, the light in the park where Tom's family picnics, this light has of course of a shimmering intensity that seems to speak of a spiritual richness imbued in nature itself. Whatever the tribulations of repression and orthodoxy that the Brothers force onto themselves, they cannot escape the rich, warm light of the sun.

Towards the climax of the film, a visiting priest, Father Marshall (Tom Keneally), arrives to hear confession and to lead a three day spiritual retreat in which the men and the boys will fast, pray and offer penance, and during which they will be forbidden to speak. In a perfectly wordless scene, young Tom is sitting on the jetty, as contemplative and silent as all the men and youths around him, and he throws a pebble into the lake. The sound of the splash, the blue-silver ripples of the water, the sun's rays shimmering on the lake's surface, all this beauty brings a smile to Tom's lips. He throws in another stone, then another. Another boy begins to do the same. Soon the world is full of the sound of splashing and giggles. A boy falls into the water with a resounding splash and the boys burst into uncontrollable laughing.

There is nothing in this sequence that is blasphemous, no sense of mocking the meditation and the retreat. It is simply that light and nature refuse to be tamed, refuse to bow to the reverences and requirements of religion—just as Tom's body, his pissing secreting growing *natural* body, refuses to be tamed. Brother Sebastian (Charles McCallum), the old man we saw at the beginning of the film, says of Tom that he has a 'smile that will take you halfway around the world'. That eager open smile is also a kind of light.

Light saturates the film, and it will be memories of light that will remain: the red and amber and dying green tussle of leaves skipping in the wind; the boys' naked bodies swimming in the water; the way the dark corridors are illuminated by shafts of golden sun. But there is darkness in the film as well, and it is of such a pitch of black that everything within this darkness becomes hidden and dank.

A group of Tom's peers, led by the obsessive, bespectacled Turner (Michael David), have become involved in fundamentalist purification rites aimed at bringing them to that ecstatic state in which the material body has been left behind. Tom is asked to join in with the boys in these extreme rites. In the night's darkness he creeps through the trees and stumbles across Turner and two other boys naked in a grotto, whipping themselves in a frenzy of ecstasy, denial and repression. Tom is chased by the boys but he slips past their arms and is saved by Fitz (John Diedrich), his older mate. (Fitz has warned Tom about Turner's near psychotic religiosity, and Tom adores Fitz and looks up to him; Fitz's eventual expulsion will lead to Tom's decision to abandon the school and his religious vocation.) Tom and Fitz then stand by the edge of the lake and whisper into the night.

The preceding scenes in the grotto have played in absolute darkness except for the flash of candlelight illuminating Turner's sado-masochistic rites. Darkness still enfolds Fitz and Tom, but a gentle suggestion of moonlight makes their faces distinct and visible again. Saved from the extreme perversions of the darkness, light and water again offer calm and order.

What did this all mean to me? *The Devil's Playground* was to remain vivid for me as a film that acknowledged and condoned my emerging sexuality, in fact, seemed to delight in the body's need for wanking, sex and pleasure. It was also to remain vivid for years as a film that confirmed my growing distrust for the development of my masculinity and my desire. I read into Tom Allen everything I wished I was, but I feared, I was terrified, that I was really Turner: ugly, possessed by a dangerous and diseased sexuality. The crazy religious rites corresponded to my own battles to eliminate homosexuality physically, materially from the body: ripping my skin, to get at the disease, to flush it out. Brother Victor thunders that the school 'is a breeding ground for bloody poofters', in a flash of anger at the repressions Catholicism forced on the boys. This is the line from the film that I remember most intensely.

I physically jumped in my seat at the contempt and horror in his expression, in his voice. In later years, as we will see, I was to return to this moment, the Brothers playing billiards, discussing the body and sex, and I was to actively refute this moment of virulent homosexual panic: I was to read it differently.

But I was not able to do this at thirteen. I was untrained, inexperienced in the critical role of cinema going and I took everything at face value. It was an exciting time. I was opening myself up to film experiences that I knew most of my mates had no idea about. But I was also opening up myself to anxieties and terrors. I feared that, like Turner, it was to the abyss of darkness, the refusal of light, that I was heading. Turner dies in the film. His body is found in the cold, freezing lake. He thought that his religious purifications were leading him to a point where he could withstand and defy the deathly cold of the winter water.

Death: was this where I was heading? Remember, this is the late 1970s, when the experience of being gay is still largely illegal, distasteful and sickening even to those of us who are homosexual ourselves, possibly doubly so. Remember too, that I am locked in a confusion where Turner becomes one of the few representations of perversion I know. No matter how ugly he is as a character, he will stay with me as a confirmation of very existence itself—which is not to say that I should not have been allowed to view the film. What would have helped would have been a mate or an adult who could have led me through it, allowed me to express some of my confusion and terror. I don't want to make light of how overwhelming the desire to kill my instincts was at time (which is why Turner's perverted rites made such perfect sense to me)— yet the will to live, the same will which demands of Tom's body that it piss and come, was active and alive in me.

This will to survive meant that I was determined to not identify myself with the 'death' represented by Turner. So I imbued a peripheral character, Tom's shy gawky friend, Waite, with a history and a psychology that, in subsequent viewings, I understood were not there in the character at all. Waite's sexuality is benign and innocent. His attempts to get his mate Tom to pull him off are a running gag throughout the film. When Tom finally agrees to being 'conquered' by him, Waite is so ignorant of the functioning of sex and his body that he has to be informed of ejaculation, a notion that repels him and scares him. His desire is child-like, presented in the film as pre-sexual rather than homosexual, a matter of affection and filial bonding not yet contaminated by the secretions and liquids of actual sex.

But what I read into Waite's character was a counter to Turner's dark perversity. I imagined a life for him. His nervousness and giggling were not only the remnants of childhood. It marked his being an outsider to the school environment. For years, I assumed his character was Eastern European or Slavic, but there is nothing in the script itself to indicate this. I wanted him to be a 'wog'. This deliberate 'misreading' of the character taught me something about the important critical activity of sometimes opposing the filmmakers' insistence that 'it is not in the film'. Of course, this is not how I understood it as a teenager. All I knew then was that I too had a 'dark' and dirty secret that did not allow me to fully be the kind of male that Tom Allen was. Waite's foolish, clumsy sexuality was preferable to Turner's burdensome and ill perversions.

At thirteen, the Brothers, as adults, seemed a lifetime away. It was the boys who made an impression on me. I think this was also a reflection of my inability at the time to identify at all with the Catholicism of the characters. I may have been trapped within a fire-and-brimstone conception of God, but I had no intention of the clerical life. The Brothers entered my imaginings only as figures of lust. For years after seeing *The Devil's Playground* I wanted to fuck Nick Tate. It is telling that I felt less guilt over fantasising about him than I did about fantasising over Simon Burke or Alan Cinis. What was forbidden was the thought of sex among my peers. That was strictly a no-no. Sex with adult men seemed not only desirable but much less fraught, much less chaotic, much less dangerous.

But that was at thirteen. I was twenty one when I saw the film again. This time the light and the dark still made an impression. But I was now to find myself fixated, disturbed, confronted by the men.

'This is a breeding ground for bloody poofters': Brother James (Peter Cox) and Brother Victor (Nick Tate) escape from the seminary and go to the footy.

2

Two years after *The Devil's Playground*, Fred Schepisi completed *The Chant of Jimmie Blacksmith*. It is tempting, in order to convey the effect this motion picture has on me—and still does—to argue that it is the greatest Australian feature film ever made. However, I am suspicious of such grand critical statements as they assume equal standards against widely differing genres; such statements don't allow for the qualifications of time and therefore relevance. But each revisit to the film has deepened my admiration and fascination with the work. *The Chant of Jimmie Blacksmith*, based on a novel by Tom Keneally, which is itself based on the true story of a young Aboriginal man who murdered a white settler family on the eve of Federation, has the tragic weight and lyricism of folk balladry.[5] I think it is one of the great film works about colonial displacement; it conveys both the vastness and the insanity of the subject.

The Western is heavily identified as a Hollywood genre, so much so that even the magnificent Sergio Leone epics require their protagonists to be Yanks or Mexicans, that genre studies by and large ignore the indigenous 'frontier' works of Australia and New Zealand, and of Latin America. Reflecting different patterns of settlement, different relationships to colonisation and the conquering of land and its people, it could be argued that the

Australian Western, if it exists as such at all, has not been a repository of conservative mythic archetypes as is the case with the classic Hollywood Western. Instead, it has always signified certain anxieties and terrors that white Australians have held about the outback.

It is certainly true that in my very early childhood the Australian film that made the greatest impression on me was Peter Dodds' *Lost in the Bush*, a film which followed the increasingly desperate situation of young children lost in the unforgiving outback bush. For a long time I thought my terror of the bush had to do with my being a migrant proletariat child. Certainly, as far as the stories we were told at school and viewed on our televisions, from the writings of Henry Lawson to the adventures of Skippy the bush kangaroo, I was instructed to believe that Australians were a largely rural people. If the Australian Western does not function with the clear set of genre tropes, situations and characters as does the Western of the United States, I believe it nevertheless exists. From historic television series such as *Ben Hall* and *Against the Wind*, to movies as disparate as George Miller's *The Man from Snowy River* and Tom Cowan's *Journey Among Women*, there is a clear body of Australian work which takes as its theme the interaction of the (largely) European settler with the frontier outback environment.[6]

There is also an earlier tradition that I imbibed through a steady diet of television viewing. These were old-timer movies featuring Chips Rafferty and a cast of identical blonde beauties—who spoke a plum-in-the-mouth version of the Australian accent which I had never heard in the real world, but who also seemed capable of defeating droughts, poisonous snakes and malcontent sheep shearers with a haughty ease. The names of these beauties and the titles of the movies in which they appeared have been obliterated from my memory. What cannot be forgotten is the sense of the vastness of the flat Australian desert landscape, the harsh intensity of our sunlight. This is the mythological terrain which we Australians absorb as intrinsic to nationhood. Even though the majority of us are urban and we wouldn't know what the fuck to do with a cow or a witchetty grub, this mythos (to a large extent) plays a determining role in how we understand our identity and our sense of place.

Alongside the stoic settlers and the unforgiving terrain, instead of the noble Red Indian warrior, white Australians have substituted their own colonial revision. 'Our' savage is not an expert warrior but a spiritual guide. This renders the Aboriginal civilisation timeless yet unthreatening when situated in the primordial outback (and conversely poisoned, corrupted and dangerous when relocated to the white urban city or to the fringes of a township).

So popular is this archetype, so endearing, so emasculated from history, that it has crossed beyond our borders. We have had Germans such as Werner Herzog (*Where the Green Ants Dream*) and Wim Wenders (*Until the End of the World*) place their faith in the Aborigine when it comes to the demise of the planet. And we have had Aboriginal spirits guide the astronauts in Philip Kaufman's *The Right Stuff*. This identification of Aboriginality with mysticism is shown most nakedly in Peter Weir's goth-apocalyptic *The Last Wave*. Aborigines have spiritual knowledge and insight that the European has lost. *The Last Wave*, however, also indicates a certain terror and fear being expressed by white Australians about the bush; a fear of what is buried beneath the desert landscape, a terror that death awaits in this harsh interior. This fear of the bush (mirrored in literature in D. H. Lawrence's 1923 novel, *Kangaroo*) suggests that there is an ambivalence to frontier mythology in Australia.[7]

It is in this context that *The Chant of Jimmie Blacksmith* delivered a swift sharp blow to our faces. It seems impossible to convey to a contemporary audience the effect of this film on an audience in 1978, at least on a member of the white audience such as myself. The ignorance of the majority of Australians back then to the rapacious, exterminating impulse of British colonialism was woeful, was shameful. Spiritual nobility is there in the film, but it is arguably too high a price to pay for the desecration of culture and the resultant material suffering and poverty. Poor Jimmie Blacksmith keeps making his accommodations to white demands. He bows and serves and obeys but to no avail. The rancid self-righteous hatred underpinning their contempt of his skin and his kin cannot be alleviated. When Jimmie strikes back, by bringing the axe onto the plump, fresh faces of his farmer bosses' porcelain white wives, mothers and children, the violence is shocking, short-lived and explosive. My guts churned but I was also extremely elated.

I'm sure that the filmmakers had no clue that the violence, the Old Testament justice, would inspire such happiness in a young adolescent wog boy in the audience. Jimmie might be an Aborigine and I, a Greek-Australian, but his attempts to be 'white' mirrored my own grappling with identity and 'Australianness'. When Jimmie takes the axe to the white women and children, these spouses and offspring of the Scots and Irish, I understood every blow. *The Chant of Jimmie Blacksmith* is not a film that lends itself to simplistic moral categorisation. Jimmie's contempt for his own Indigenous background makes him an anti-hero for *all* Australian audiences (though it's precisely because of this ambiguity that I identified so strongly with his violence).

I should not have seen *The Chant of Jimmie Blacksmith*. It was restricted to adults and I was not yet fifteen. But luckily my father made no stink about buying me a ticket, and my fortunate Mediterranean propensity to early and rapid physical development either fooled the ushers or they really did not give a damn. Of course, it did nothing but good that I saw such a film, in the same way it was fortunate that I had snuck into *The Devil's Playground* a few years earlier. Firstly, almost inadvertently, it allowed me to come to an understanding of film artistry through a distinctly Australian expression and context. Both films are confident and assured works, both films also are exemplary collaborative efforts—but there is a world of difference between the personal, intimate adolescent recollections of *The Devil's Playground* and the grand sweep of *The Chant of Jimmie Blacksmith*. In a sense they gave me permission to imagine wildly, to be introspective or to be grand in my dreaming and fantasies.

My affirming the importance of *The Devil's Playground* being an Australian film is not simply nationalist rhetoric. As a teenager, watching Schepisi's films allowed me to imagine one day translating my own stories for the screen. I remember distinctly that for many years I could only imagine 'Hollywood' films. It was not till I recognised a tradition of Australian and non-English language cinema that I was able to create distinctly Australian scenarios and storyboards in my exercise books. Why didn't I imagine films in Greek settings? Maybe because by my teens I had recognised that Greek cinema did not have legitimacy, was too populist, even in the context of European 'art' cinema (which largely meant Italian, French, British and German film). In making me react to Australian history, to Australian light and sounds, Schepisi's films assisted me in resisting the Yankee colonisation of my imagination.

With adolescence and my hesitant lurchings towards adulthood, I began to immerse myself in film. Am I simply being nostalgic, or is it true that never again will there be a time so delightful, so precious, like the honeymoon period of first love? I was being deliciously seduced, royally fucked by film itself. And like a young kid discovering the joys of onanism, I could not leave film alone. I was going to the pictures three or four times a week, spending all my pocket money on the movies, spending hours on the floor of the local suburban library reading anything I could on film. There is something about the film buff experience that is definitely connected to sexual inexperience and longing. Films were an erotic domain in which I was not some introverted, overweight wog kid but in which I could project myself, fantasise, that I was a sophisticated intellectual. I think this adolescent longing and sexual anxiety underlies much of the obsessive behaviour of the 'film buff', and the 'music fan'.[8]

For the young queer buff, there is another level of safety, an easing of anxiety, in the ability of film to blur distinctions of gender and class identification. An older generation of homosexuals had constructed an emotional calendar defined by La Streisand's career: I would cut out Jill Clayburgh's face from *Movie* magazine, Jane Fonda from *Time*, Jean Seberg from some old movie book I had desecrated in the library. I'd put their faces on my school folders and carry them around. Everyone, they must have guessed I was a fag!

But it was not only arrested development that made me mad for the movies. If it had been only that, I don't think it would have been an obsession that remains with me today. The movie going that I was experiencing opened up a world of critical knowledge, philosophy and history that simply was not part of the curriculum of a 1970s Australian adolescence. *The Chant of*

Jimmie Blacksmith taught me something significant and crucial about Australian history—this was the dizzying, shattering effect of movie going for me. In a short burst of years I had discovered Bergman and through his films explored my own disillusionment with God. I learnt of Marxist hopes through Bertolucci and modernism through Godard. I did not have a classical background behind me, I could not rely on either familial or scholastic encouragement for intellectual knowledge. Film provided this for me.

Of course, not just film: books were also part of this exhilarating ride. I saw Warren Beatty's *Reds* time and time again, feverishly casting myself in the role of a revolutionary hero, but it was not until I read John Reed and Emma Goldman themselves, Lenin and his critics, that I was able to understand something about the Russian revolution other than it being a romance.[9] Film could introduce me to worlds and history, could overpower me, give me a sense of smells and place, but on their own films cannot enhance critical awareness and rarely can give an audience a sense of the complexity and breadth of an issue or an historical event. Possibly books, on their own, are not enough either—but the compulsive linearity of montage, the rapid rhythms of film, do not allow space for reflection or argument. This is a generalisation for there are exceptions: much of Godard's work and the film essays of Chris Marker; Agnes Varda's *The Gleaners and I*; Claude Lanzmann's *Shoah*. There is literature which reads like film: J. D. Salinger's *The Catcher in the Rye*; Brett Easton Ellis' *Less Than Zero*; and from an earlier era, Emily Bronte's *Wuthering Heights*.[10] But I can't think of a non-fiction book that feels like cinema. And, maybe I am forgetting some, but I can't think of any film with a fictional narrative that can be experienced as measured argument. To put it bluntly, unlike a book, you can't put a film down and reflect, look up a reference or allow the space for distance and contemplation.

It seems important to stress this in a context where the divide between something called 'low' and 'high' culture has been increasingly undermined—but unfortunately it seems to have been overtaken by a deliberately anti-elitist yet moronic populism. If I hear another film student rave on to me about the importance of entertainment and their 'boredom' with seriousness, I think I'll scream. (Their films invariably make me scream, in anguish more than anger.) Sure, in my early years of cinema going, everything was new and most films seemed exciting. It was easy to fall in love with a piece of film because we had no idea if it was derivative or stale. But you move on. To make cultural illiteracy and historical amnesia a goal is ludicrous and, I would suggest, the real elitism. I count myself incredibly fortunate that I was discovering cinema at the time when the Movie Brats' films were being shown on television—Coppola, Scorsese, De Palma, et al.—and when the inner-city art house cinemas were still playing retrospectives of 'classic', experimental and 'difficult' films.[11]

I also count myself incredibly fortunate that I started reading and reading voraciously from an early age. It got me through school and it got me to university. I was to find out that academic life was a limitation and that it had the effect of alienating me from my familial and cultural roots. But it also gave me access to mobility and opportunities that my parents and their peers had never taught me about because they never knew they existed.

I never went through a phase of 'dumbing down', of believing that reading and learning to articulate yourself was a 'wank' or a waste of time. That's because I knew relatives who were illiterate—who were never going to go to school, because they were born female or lived in the southern Mediterranean in the mid-twentieth century, where poverty was endemic. At thirteen I had responded instinctively to Tom Allen's escape from the seminary. Films, books, they were my escape, and they were also my access to a wider life. If I sound harsh in deploring the pose of anti-elitism struck by many contemporary film students and critics, it is because these largely bourgeois students and artists have not come from worlds narrowed by lack of opportunity, worlds in which excess of choice is not known.

I needed film to be more than entertainment. I was hoping that films would expose the very things I was beginning to question and to be angry about.

I want to state very carefully and very insistently that this anger and questioning, this political awareness, predated any academic training. Its genesis was in my family's own histories— they were, after all, people who had lived through World War II, the Greek Civil War, an earlier Balkan tragedy.

Film certainly contributed to this consciousness. I could not be introduced to the great panorama of European cinema post-1968 without being immersed in a sometimes didactic, sometimes revolutionary, sometimes woefully self-indulgent political cinema. I'm talking about Ermanno Olmi's *The Tree of Wooden Clogs* and Godard's *Weekend* (which I first saw scratched and faded to pink, the rickety sounds emanating from the 16 mm projector giving me a headache). I'm talking about seeing Bertolucci's *1900* and thinking that it shat all over *Gone With the Wind*. Sure, I was arrogant and in many ways it was laughable. How much of what I was seeing made any sense to me? Much of it didn't, some of it may have even bored me to sleep occasionally but what I am insisting on celebrating here is the urge to learn, the legitimacy of scholarship. This is the tradition from which being a film buff and a music aficionado emerges.

How was I going to approach a film like *The Devil's Playground* again, a film that had mattered so much to me when I was younger? Was it going to remind me of the pretty private school boys and girls who dominated university life, whose very timbre of voice and swagger spoke of wealth and therefore self-assurance?

In 1989 I was sharing a house in Melbourne with my lover and two friends. We had a conversation one night about the films in our lives. I was reminded of the first Schepisi film. I decided to find it on video and to watch it by myself, distrusting that communal moment when someone, unknowingly, dismisses or mocks something that means a life to you. How was I going to view *The Devil's Playground* ten years on?

I was no longer a young boy in a migrant, prole world. I was educated, I knew something about film, I thought I knew something about the world, what really mattered.

I had a chip on my shoulder to prove it.

1989

This is a breeding ground for bloody poofters. Brother Victor

The Devil's Playground begins with a title. It is 'Autumn, 1953'. It is a seemingly innocent title, an assuring note of nostalgia. Schepisi is an astounding master of the past—like the one filmmaker whom he most resembles in his mise en scène and his eclectic choice of material, Louis Malle. In both *The Chant of Jimmie Blacksmith* and *The Devil's Playground*, the past is rendered shockingly modern; the very clothes of the performers seem real and lived in. It's the same intelligence at work in Malle's *Lacombe, Lucien* and *Murmur of the Heart*, where the moral compromises and brutalities of the war years are rendered immediate, where the stately decor and

His first kiss: Tom (Simon Burke) and Lynette (Danee Lindsay).

accoutrements of the period films are less vital than the flesh and features of people.

Compare Schepisi's mastery at creating sensual lived-in worlds, worlds that smell and stink and sweat, to the formality of Bruce Beresford's work in *The Getting of Wisdom* and *Breaker Morant*; the first, like *The Devil's Playground*, also a memoir of school and adolescence, the latter, like *The Chant of Jimmie Blacksmith*, a work of violent reprisal in war. I remember the stiff period clothes of *The Getting of Wisdom* and little else. I remember thinking that the girl at the centre of that film belonged neither to the nineteenth century nor the twentieth. And I felt that the tragedy in *Breaker Morant* was forced and schematic. Do we need to strip the ruthless truths from the historic Morant to argue that his execution was unjust and convenient? Or are we to believe that if he was truly a racist, an expedient execution would have indeed been warranted? There is no such easy moral plastering in Jimmie Blacksmith's story. The women and children he slaughters are, in terms of law, innocent. Maybe this was the reason why the film was a commercial failure on its release. Its disquieting power has to do with the suggestion that on some ethical level, if Jimmie's blows with the axe are understood as an act of war, his murders are neither evil nor unjust.

Tom Allen's fears and anxieties feel right. They feel like 1953. As the video began and I remembered that at thirteen I had overlooked that it was set in the past, I had to reflect on what that implied for the safety and cloistering of my own boyhood.

It is not a condescending portrait of adolescence that Schepisi offers—far from it. At times Tom's dilemmas about his inability to stop wanking or wetting his bed may be funny, but they never undermine his frisky good-naturedness. It struck me forcibly, on revisiting the film, that there is never an anxiety for the audience that Tom will be damaged or silenced by his experience at the Catholic seminary. When I was a teenager, I did not realise this optimism consciously but I must have done so instinctively. However, back then at thirteen, I had also instinctively assumed that it was Tom's heterosexuality, the *naturalism* of his sexuality, that allowed him this freedom. Back then, I thought the film was showing me an alternative to the dark sin of my body and its desires: Tom's natural, almost smiling 'straightness'.

Is this all in the film or is it in my imagination?

Let's just proceed and trust me in assuming that it is both. There are silences in *The Devil's Playground* but should we leave these silences mute? There is, after all, no 'gay' character as such in this film. Only one desultory mutual jack off between two school boys.[12] On a second viewing of the film, concentrating on the men whose very vocation is dependent on the silences of meditation and contemplation, it strikes me that these Brothers are quiet about many things.

Australians are said to be silent about many things. Australian culture offers reticence as a virtue. You hear it in pubs; it's in the rhetoric of politicians, that in this 'new world' there is none of the bloody history of the 'old world'. Conflict arises and this silence is upset when Australians are reminded of a more complex and less edifying history, when something like *The Chant of Jimmie Blacksmith* reflects back on a legacy of blood and massacre.

What does any of this have to do with *The Devil's Playground*? Surely setting the film in 1953, in those calm, quiet years after World War II, asks us to ignore politics, history and change. *The Devil's Playground* is silent about politics. In fairness, shouldn't I be as well? The reality, however, is that I am an 'outsider' Australian—an Australian who grew up with politics at the kitchen table, an Australian not born into a culture of Anglo reticence but whose identity in part emerged from the savage history of my parents' experience in World War II and the Greek Civil War. The Brothers and their students might be silent about politics, but that silence was not an option for me.

In 1953, within the ranks of the Australian Labor Party (ALP), a momentous political struggle was under way which would eventually result in the party being torn in two. The labour movement had been divided four years earlier when the conservative Liberal Party, under the prime ministership of Robert Menzies, had tried to pass legislation banning the Communist Party of Australia. A referendum in 1951 to make the law constitutionally valid was only narrowly beaten.

Cold War anti-communist hysteria was destroying unity and cohesion in the ALP. A Catholic anti-communist minority, centered around an organisation called the Movement (officially the Catholic Social Studies Movement), began to actively campaign to limit and undermine the influence of alleged communists within the Labor Party. Though never official, the Catholic Church gave tacit support to this opposition. The Movement worked with the 'Groupers', anti-communist industrial groups in the unions set up by the ALP itself, in order to counter communism in the union movement. Working across the union movement, the Groupers managed to win control of a minority of unions.

The Groupers and the Movement were hostile to the then leader of the Labor Party, Dr. H. V. Evatt, arguing that he was soft on communism for opposing Menzies's attempt to ban the Communist Party. Evatt, in turn, blamed the Movement's divisive agitation for the Labor Party's 1954 electoral loss. The unions attached to the Groupers were formally expelled by the ALP in 1954 and the following year, the expelled Victorian members formed the Australian Labor Party (non-communist) which was incorporated into the nationwide Democratic Labor Party in 1957.

This bitter ideological clash and power struggle, particularly virulent in Victoria, was not limited to politicians. Priests thundered about the threat of communism from their pulpits, it split the union movement and it caused a distrust of Catholicism that was still evident in schoolyard taunts twenty years later. (At my old primary school we were all Labor supporters except for those from Irish Catholic backgrounds—their parents had not forgotten the split.) The political antagonisms of the Cold War had their obvious role to play in the split but what is important to understand for the purpose of this book is that the Catholic Church—its clergy, its membership, its intellectuals—were all affected by it.

The DLP's base and largest electoral support was within Victoria. In subsequent elections, the DLP directed its preferences to the non-Labor conservative parties. Effectively, this split resulted in the ALP failing to gain power in Australia for close to a quarter of a century. This situation remained unchanged until 1972, when the increasing secularisation of society (which included Catholic dissatisfaction with church teachings on divorce and contraception) and increased opposition to Australian involvement in the Vietnamese Civil War led to the election of Labor's Gough Whitlam as prime minister.

In the post-Cold War era it is difficult to convey the explosive divisions generated by this split. Every weekend, Bob Santamaria, the most eloquent spokesperson for the Movement and its successor, the National Civic Council, hosted a five-minute diatribe on commercial television in Melbourne, a diatribe which preceded *World Championship Wrestling*, which was what we all *really* wanted to watch.

Now, I was just a kid and Santamaria made no attempt to sweeten his message and make it palatable to the children and migrant labourers who were wrestling's biggest fans. Dad would often throw things at the television when he was on. I assumed he was just another conservative capitalist who hated workers and therefore, in the emotionally charged rhetoric of the Cold

War, I had to hate him right back.[13] I picked up that Santamaria, his bald head bopping earnestly, his voice seemingly close to emotional exhaustion, approved of Australian involvement in the Vietnamese Civil War and that he thought Gough Whitlam was a secret communist. Given that I learned from an early age that Australians were fucking mad for sending troops to an Asian war just to do the United States' bidding, and given that Whitlam was the one mortal deity whose name my mother would deign to utter alongside Jesus Christ Pantocrator, Emperor of the Universe,[14] it is not surprising, for me, that Santamaria and the DLP came to represent the most regressive and destructive aspect of conservative politics.

I, fortunately, did not get raised an anti-Catholic, and the split was explained to me as being much more about the relationship between communism and capitalism than about religion. Back in the 1970s, the reality was that communism was not simply something espoused by restless bourgeois students. My memories of boyhood include many evenings falling asleep in Mum's arms while around the kitchen table there were heated discussions about socialism, unionism and capital. Many of these factory workers were communists or, at the very least, sympathised with communist politics and agendas. There were certainly enough perceived communists in Victoria in the 1950s to cause a split within the Labor Party.

It is 1953 and the seminary Tom attends is just outside Melbourne, in rural Victoria. Though the Brothers will discuss their differences and antagonisms to God and their Catholic creed, not one of them mentions the bitter and tumultuous events that will result in the split. Maybe it was true that in certain Catholic orders the worldly and material concerns of politics were not seen as important enough to engage the interests of true believers. The Brothers in this film do argue, do engage in sometimes antagonistic discussions about sex and about faith, but the undeniably real political machinations of the Catholic Church are never referred to. It is as if the seminary itself is isolated, cut off from the rest of society and only the concerns of adolescence are topics of discussion. The one directly political utterance comes not from the men or the boys, but from the frazzled Irish housekeeper (an over-the-top Sheila Florance). She reminds the Brothers that even though there is no culture more faithful than the Irish, there has 'never been an Irish Pope, has there Father?'.

In a 1993 television interview Fred Schepisi talks of the autobiographical nature of *The Devil's Playground*.[15] A child of Polish immigrants, he attended a Catholic boarding school. He, too, left school in his teens, in his case to begin work in an advertising agency. There is a rugged charm to Schepisi: he, too, has a smile that has obviously taken him halfway around the world. Simon Burke is prettier, but Tom's larrikin straightforwardness is visible in the film director. In his interviews Fred Schepisi seems to deliberately eschew controversial or complex readings of his films. *The Devil's Playground* may deal with the anguish of repressed men but the anguish we witness is ultimately distanced, detached. It is as if we are viewing the events in the film through an adolescent boy's prurient eyes. This is a boy who doesn't care for discussions of politics. He wants to know about erections, pulling himself off. And what God thinks of all this.

Am I saying that the film disappointed me when I saw it again? No, far from it.

In 1983 I had seen John Duigan's haunting adolescent memoir, *The Year My Voice Broke,* and I had thought that it was a finer film.

Seeing *The Devil's Playground* again, however, made me realise the limitations of such comparisons. How do you make a call between lyrical and earthy depictions of the past? Do you argue for the lightness of memory in *The Devil's Playground* or for the pain of remembrance in *The Year My Voice Broke*? They are both bewitching films, both remarkably free of condescension to their adolescent characters.

What did strike me on placing them alongside each other was the question of whether this was, finally, the terrain to which Australian filmmaking was best suited: explorations of the past, reminiscences of children. This seemed to correspond to what I was discovering as underlying much of Australian culture: a fierce dislike of intellectual debate and argument, the 'silence' to which I've referred above. This silence commands that bloody violence is preferable to a political disagreement. In our persistent urge to see ourselves as blessed, 'the lucky country', we ask of ourselves and of our artists to be unconcerned with the folly of politics and to sanitise our history.

There are exceptions and, of course, these are some of my favourite of Australian films—*Ghosts...of the Civil Dead*, *Don's Party*, *The Chant of Jimmie Blacksmith*, *Evil Angels*, *BeDevil*—films whose canvas is vast, films unafraid of speaking about and to and through the culture. They are imaginatively rich, intellectually dense, as well as being emotionally and morally complex. The Australian characters that emerge from these films are not merely 'laconic', 'ocker', a 'bloke' or a 'sheila' (or if some of them are, as in *BeDevil*, they are juxtaposed against the 'ghosts', 'deviants' and 'outsiders' who also populate the Australian landscape). In these films the harsh instances of misogyny, violence and racism are not easily reducible to stereotypes of good and bad. They are films not afraid of failing, not afraid at times to court excess or pretension, and most impressively of all in the Australian context, they are truly adult, mature works. They were also, all of them, not popular successes.

No, *The Devil's Playground* did not disappoint me on a second viewing. It has a much more intimate canvas than the films I have mentioned above, but it shares their emotional complexity. Even at their most punishing or self-deluded, none of the characters are brutes. Tom still seemed heroic in his disastrous attempts to convert his heathen body, and even when diluted by the scale of the television screen, by the coarseness with which video renders the image, the light and colours of the film were still luminous. The whole of the film, except for those moments when the perversions of the night eliminate all light, still shimmered like water.

Seeing again the scenes amongst the students, I was once more knocked out by the small scene in the woodshed where Tom and Waite fiddle nervously with their hands. The talk of erections and dick size is smutty, they giggle and lop off their words, but I don't know of another more exquisite rendering of the way sexual energy literally seems to pour forth from a boy's body. At this viewing I was freed from having to deny the intensity of my gaze: the boys are beautifully lit and filmed, their awkward youthful male prettiness is, paradoxically, both erotic and chaste. Whether naked in the water, running in their sports kits in the rain, at assembly or at rest, identical in the blue and grey of their uniform, their white flesh, the sheen of their eyes, their mottled blonde curls or their jet-black Irish locks all seem to glisten, to be vibrant. Even though they are pock-marked, pimpled, clumsy and shy, when the light falls on them it reveals only beauty.

The men, however, are trapped in their dark robes. Whereas the boys are often seen running, walking, embracing the vast Australian outdoors, the Brothers are viewed from behind the glass and walls of the seminary. The boys are woken every morning by a harsh bell and they cannot wait to escape their dormitories and be in the clear, crisp air. The men congregate in their common room, drinking whisky, playing billiards. Their conversation, again and again, comes back to the burden of their Catholic faith. Old Brother Sebastian, descending into senility, interrupts the other men to soliloquise on the joys of self-pleasure: 'What's so wrong with masturbation, anyway? If you don't do it yourself, it comes out of its own accord.' He finishes by crying out, 'We're all mad … What if God isn't there? We'll hate ourselves then'.

The rest of the Brothers ignore him, in part because the self-hatred is already eating away at them. You can't help feeling that in part they are locking themselves into the confines of their common room because it keeps them away from the temptations of the boys—I mean sexual temptation as well as simply the temptations of procrastination, levity and selfishness which are prerogatives of youth. The contradictory consequences of this repression are visible in the differing attitudes of Brothers Victor and Francine to their Catholic faith. The former, who is handsome and blokey, his vernacular peppered with Australian slang, is the most vocal of the men against the repressive rules of the institution. It is he who condemns the seminary as a 'breeding ground for bloody poofters'. Brother Francine is his opposite. Gangly and aloof, his vocal inflections pompous and aristocratic, he is the most diligent in applying the strict doctrinaire rules of Catholicism to each boy, and to himself.

Both Brothers are being eaten away by their torturous attempts to deny the very bodily liberty that Tom cannot contain. In one of

The prison of faith: The Brothers in their common room.

the film's pivotal scenes, three of the Brothers, Victor, Francine and the younger James (Peter Cox), take leave from the seminary and venture to Melbourne. Francine visits a suburban pool and allows himself to indulge in viewing the naked and near-naked bodies of the women and men in the pool and change rooms. It is the film's most erotic sequence. The variety of bodies—fat, thin, old, young, hairy, smooth—are all filmed equally generously so that the flesh, like the flesh of the schoolboys, seems alive with colour and energy. As he immerses himself in the swimming pool, peering at the full bosoms of the young women, Francine's face is a study in carnal agony.

For Brothers Victor and James, temptation proves to be much more prosaic; their activities identify them as quintessential 'ordinary men'. They promptly pocket their clerical collars on this day of 'freedom' in the city. We see them at the footy, drinking, betting, and finally continuing drinking at a pub. Two women who work in a factory make eyes at the two men. Victor, drunk, flirts with the women while a scared, or reluctant, James makes his escape. There is a cut from the pub to a shot from the car interior in which Brother James has retired to sleep off his drunkenness. Victor runs staggering up the street, opens the door and gets behind the wheel: 'They nearly had me.'

It is during the retreat, when all members of the community are forbidden to speak, that Brother Francine's expedition to Melbourne returns as a waking nightmare. Alone in his celibate single bed he fantasises about a group of young nymphs dragging him down into the blue water. They are touching him, feeling him up, fondling his naked body. It is a startling scene: wordless, a siren's water ballet. It is the only time we see any of the men naked, see *their* flesh. While the sirens have bodies which are lush and sexy and full, the Brother's body appears limp, lit so that its whiteness is for once closer to decay and death than it is to life. Cutting back and forth from the nightmare to the lonely, frightened man in the bed, we understand that whatever awaits the Brother in the afterlife, this life as a man of God has been Hell. After the retreat has finished, and Father Marshall has departed, Francine in a drunken fury reminds the Brothers that 'the body will not be denied'. It is a momentary indiscretion.

When we next see him he is again attired in the stiff black cloth, buttoned from the neck to the ground, reminding the boys of the strict terrible rules of God's kingdom.

Brother Francine's behaviour, whatever one might think of him as a character, is at least consistent. It is the figure of Brother Victor that is perplexing. In a bizarre scene, just before commencing the vow of silence, Victor confesses to Father Marshall how he cannot live outside the community of the church. He talks of 'affecting some change for the good', and proudly declares that 'I am good with the boys'. This avowal of the strength and nourishment he receives from his fellow Brothers rings hollow; the volatile, frustrated masculinity expressed through Nick Tate's characterisation of the Brother is hardly a portrayal of a man at rest in the peaceful, ethereal world of spiritual retreat. He is not even a particularly good teacher. In the classroom scenes early in the film, his teaching methods are shown to be tired and unilluminating: the boys are barely registering interest.

The only moments in which we see Brother Victor at peace are in the camaraderie he shares with Brother James. The younger man offers Victor affection. The factory women nearly 'had' Victor; there seemed never any danger that they would have the younger Brother James. He hastily makes his retreat from the pub. Victor's meaning in confessing his desire for the seminary's fraternity of men is made more ambiguous when the jovial, friendly Father Marshall is revealed to be a fiery traditionalist, a believer in the Old Testament's retributive God. Tom Keneally delivers a suitably baroque and terrifying performance in giving a sermon to the men and boys in which Hell is described in all its grizzly, lonely horror. Francine may be right to fear the sirens, but Victor's frustrations are to remain silent.

The scene between Father Marshall and Brother Victor is preceded by a sequence in which Tom's family arrive to pay him a visit and he is taken out of the school grounds to a local guesthouse. The family scenes are idyllic. Tom's family sings and goes fishing together, and there are no hints of hidden resentments. Also staying at the guesthouse are a group of schoolgirls, one of whom will form an attachment to Tom. Other guests include two young men: one, an actor and an obvious dandy and the other, an accountant. The actor attempts to entice Tom into conversation on the lawn. Tom is clearly uncomfortable. The actor mocks Tom's spiritual vocation and the boy's defence of it is half-hearted. Tom is much more interested in a couple of schoolgirls teasing him from a balcony above the lawn. Unable to restrain himself, Tom shoots off and chases the girls, much to the actor's disgust. The chase will end with Tom receiving his first kiss.

I stated above that there is no 'gay' character in *The Devil's Playground* except, possibly, the tortured Turner and two young men staying at the same hotel as Tom's parents.[16] On a second screening I was no longer so sure. Tom's heterosexuality still comes across as perfectly natural. He may piss in his bed, not know what to do with his cock, he may be serious about his wish to be a Brother, but ultimately there is a lightness, a lack of heaviness, to Tom's adolescence. He is a very fortunate young man. A beautiful girl gives him his first kiss under an earthy kaleidoscope of a forest canopy, the blood-red leaves announcing the onset of winter. It could be that it is this lightness that Brother Victor recognises and which makes him offer to assist Tom in escaping from the school. There is a heaviness to Brother Victor that mirrors the near hysterical perfectionism of Brother Francine.

They are both burdened by the cost of repressing their body, their sexual lusts. That is, of course, a problem for all the men in the seminary, but because their appetites are larger, the damage is greater.

There are Brothers who seem to have attained a level of contentment in their celibacy, faith and teaching vocation. In particular, this comes across in Jonathan Hardy's portrayal of Brother Arnold. It is as if sex has been banished so completely from consciousness that even his very body has deserted adulthood and returned to puberty. It is Brother Arnold, rather than Victor, who can make the claim that he is good with the students. When we watch Arnold kick the soccer ball amongst the boys, he seems every bit as young as they are.

In contrast, age has carved its damage across the visages of both Arthur Dignam, who plays Francine, and Nick Tate, who plays Brother Victor. It is surprising that these educated, passionate men find no time to discuss politics or the world, but *The Devil's Playground* is the world seen through a child's eye. The adults' place in the narrative is to offer Tom a vision of what he would become if he stayed on at the seminary, if he found a way of restraining his body and sexual will. Brother Francine is close to a nightmarish cartoon of what repression will do to a male. He is a ponce, and referred to as such in the film. Thin-lipped, tight-arsed, an emasculated man whose only moments of empowerment come from punishing young boys and men. It is only the dignity of Arthur Dignam's performance that arrests the comedy of Francine's persona and allows us to recognise the lustful sexual being beneath the robes. Nick Tate's warm masculinity, his very broadness, is what is at odds with the compromises that his character, Brother Victor, has made in his life. His is a body that demands sexual pleasure and a mastery of itself. This is another possible outcome for Tom Allen if he were to become a man of the cloth: caught forever in a stage of arrested development, maintaining the permanent erection and making temptation into a game.

Tom Allen is charmed. This Celtic expression seems apt for the Catholic milieu of the film. His nocturnal emissions—piss and come—may give him some anxiety but sexuality does not damage him. This is not true for Francine or Victor, certainly not true for Turner, possibly not true for Waite and Brother James. The film's refusal to articulate words for sexuality, to name the precise aspect of the body which Turner wishes to expunge, to give voice to Victor's longings, for example, allows us to read the peripheral characters in myriad ways. In fact, the only scene which illuminates sexual desire and sexual repression, Francine's afternoon of voyeurism at the pool, is one in which all bodies and both sexes appear ravishing. In this instance, the camera is bisexual. If Tom's heterosexuality is undeniable, this is not so straightforward when it comes to the other men and boys who figure prominently in the story. There may not be 'gay' characters, but there doesn't seem to be many 'straight' characters either.

When Brother Victor confesses his love for the Brothers to Father Marshall, what creates the dissonance for us as an audience is that we can't believe it. Whatever the sirens attacking Brother Victor's sleep might be, I have no doubt that they are real. His confession, therefore, seems much more a justification for why he has chosen to remain on in the seminary. Brother Victor mocks the strict disciplinarian Francine, mocks his fundamentalist faith, but Francine's convictions give meaning to the choices he has made in life. Brother Victor, however, does not obey out of faith: he obeys out of fear.

We have to intuit the reasons for Victor's fear because Schepisi shares the chasteness of the adolescent boys. On revisiting *The Devil's Playground* I was struck by how much the film mirrored the reticence and silence of the time it was made. There is much talk of sex in the film but the act of sex itself never occurs. In calling this reticence 'homophobic' I don't want to imply that there was anything malevolent in the filmmaker's intentions. Victor's frustration still makes sense to me because back in 1977, let alone back in 1953, there didn't seem to be the words to give expression to what sexuality is. Tom, who is certainly straight, could make his escape and run away. Where would a faggot Tom have gone? Or a faggot Victor?

The incident that makes Tom decide to run away from the seminary is the expulsion of his older mate, Fitz. When he demands to know where Fitz has gone, why he has been expelled, he is told firmly by a Brother that he is not to know the answer to these questions and he is to assume that from now on, Fitz is dead. This is the cruelty that sits alongside the camaraderie that Brother Victor extols as the community's finest virtue. Their faith demands that loyalty is directed always towards the institution of the church itself, the representative of God here on earth itself. This forces Tom's break with Catholicism for he is loyal to life here on earth: to his body, his prick, his mates, his family, to the taste of a girl's lips. He runs away and is discovered hitchhiking by Brother Victor and Brother James. The two men offer him a lift into the city and the last we see of Tom is his smiling face in the back seat, the sunlight reflecting on the window, his face brushed by a sea of silver leaves. In granting Tom's wish to be taken to Melbourne, it is clear that both James and Victor are acknowledging that he is right to choose freedom above faith.

What this implies for themselves, for their choices as Brothers and as men, is unclear. In this last scene from the film they are hidden from the camera. We see them only in silhouette, in darkness.

The Devil's Playground is a child's vision. The clarity and unsensational nature of its depiction of masculine adolescence arises partly, I would think, from Schepisi's ability to have imaginatively re-entered the mind of a thirteen-year-old. I can think of no other reason why this film still allowed me, at twenty-one, to vividly remember, both fondly and painfully, my own awkward adolescent past.

Lost to freedom, the adult men around Tom either retire into a version of second childhood, like Brother Arnold, or they incorporate into their faith a resigned bitterness. The Brothers are, to some extent, sentinels for a future available to Tom if he resists his body and cows to institutional discipline; so it is no wonder that what would animate the lives of these men is of no interest to the teenage boys, and was of no interest to me aged thirteen.

We hear nothing of the political splits tearing apart the Catholic community in Melbourne because it is of little interest to Tom. Watching the film again as an adult, I found myself wondering what Brother Victor would think of the split and the Movement, and I questioned why someone like him would remain in a faith he did not quite believe in. I wondered what limitations he placed on his love and affection for Brother James. Would he give him up if asked? Or would he, like Tom over Fitz, make a stand for mortal relationships?

It strikes me that Tom's decision to disobey the seminary's instructions to think of Fitz as 'dead' is precisely what liberates

Pastoral care: Brother Sebastian (Charles McCallum) encourages Tom (Simon Burke) to reconsider his vocation.

him; it is an acknowledgment that human relationships are equal to spiritual relationships. It is certainly an avowal encouraged by the dying Brother Sebastian. (In one of the movie's most tender scenes, on a balcony in the rain, Sebastian gently encourages Tom to rethink his commitment to taking up a religious life. Brother Victor may mock Francine's religiosity but finally both men are equally trapped in the monastic life; in fact, Francine may be the less self-deluded.)

I let the titles run till the end of the video. I am reminded of how much I like Bruce Smeaton's music. I light a cigarette and attempt to make sense of what I thought of *The Devil's Playground*. I have come to a point where I want Australian culture and its art to challenge me, to open my mind to ideas, my eyes and ears to new sounds and visions.

I had forgotten that the world of the film is so claustrophobic, or maybe it is only now that I realise this. There seems to be no place in the whole seminary to escape the voices of boys and men. The school environment is perfectly recreated. The question that came to me when I first ran the video—what is Tom Allen's class background?—had not been answered but, then, I had discovered that there were many things left silent in this movie. Maybe this is why Tom's realm seems so claustrophobic; there's nothing of difference, nothing of the world outside.

In the early 1970s Australian cinema experienced a period of growth, a maturation of talent at all levels of production and experiment, that gave rise to the phrase, the 'Australian renaissance'. In many ways it was. This renaissance was built on the election of a social-democratic Labor government that put an end to our involvement in the Vietnamese Civil War and a government which developed a progressive social politics that brought a conservative Anglophile Australia kicking and screaming into a multi-ethnic present.

Our films indicated the effects of some of these changes but, ultimately, they didn't find a way to communicate in a new cinematic language. Periods of renaissance in other national cinemas have resulted in radical change or experimentation with the very grammar and form of film: the experimental work created by Bolshevik film artists such as Eisenstein and Dziga Vertov in the 1920s; the re-invigoration of genre and the philosophical explorations of the French *nouvelle vague*; the humanist transformations of performance and narrative in both Italian neo-realism and post-revolutionary Iranian cinema. Australian films in the 1970s gave us Australian stories on our screens but they were told to us in forms and genres that either mirrored the entertainments of Hollywood or the aesthetics of European cinema in the 1960s.[17]

Maybe I am expecting too much from film. The Bolshevik revolution, the World Wars, the Iranian revolution: all these were grand historical events that transformed society and this was reflected in the cultural production of the artists. After all, in Australia in the 1970s, all we had was a change of government—but I believe there were possibilities for something transcendent in Australian cinema. *The Chant of Jimmie Blacksmith*, infused with savage light and filled with cruel horizons, managed to give our history of colonial exploitation and destruction the insane grand canvas it deserved.

But Australian films in the 1970s were not interested in changing the world, and Australians are best at the intimacy of the everyday. *The Devil's Playground* explores a very small moment in time but it does so with a grace and refreshing truthfulness that, I think, will make Tom Allen a permanent figure in our collective cultural landscape. The best of our filmmakers—Schepisi in *The Devil's Playground*, John Duigan in *Winter of Our Dreams* and *The Year My Voice Broke*, Ivan Sen in his short film *Tears*, and Mary Callaghan in *Greetings from Wollongong*—have created an impressive cinematic portraiture of quiet gestures and even quieter heartbreak. This is a cinema of character, fragile and tender, and it's probably the most lasting legacy of the 'Australian renaissance'. (It's certainly true that these films are blessedly free of the pomposity and old-wave classicism that I can't stand in films such as *Gallipoli*.) Am I selfish to ask for more from any national cinema?

I certainly don't want to settle for less. What I mean is: ours is not such a lucky country. Remember, I have a chip on my shoulder. That's what *The Chant of Jimmie Blacksmith* reminds us of. So does Tracey Moffatt in *BeDevil*, and in a different way, by being prepared to attempt a witnessing of the unimaginable and the unspeakable, so does Jackie Farkas in her short film *The Illustrated Auschwitz*. These films are not content with the everyday, are not content to work only with small canvases. They do not merely describe but they also transform; in Moffatt's case, she literally creates a new way of looking at the Australian landscape. These films remind us that we're part of the world and history, and that so much of the world and history is here.

I take the video out of the machine and wipe my eyes. Watching Simon Burke's face, the wide expansive grin on his freckled cheeks, watching the sun's rays beat and dance on the car windows, I was exhilarated once more that Tom Allen had chosen his freedom.

I was still in that moment. That moment was still precious.

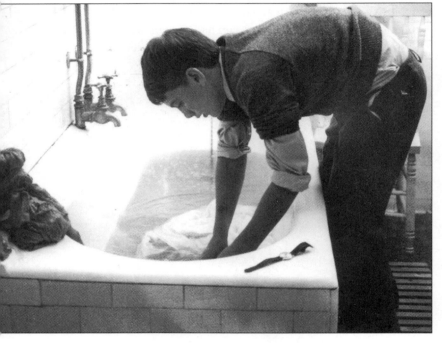

'An undisciplined mind is the devil's playground': Tom (Simon Burke)
removing the evidence of sin.

3

I never quite got film theory, to be honest. I'm not being perversely anti-intellectual here. I just never really got it. From the French semiotician Christian Metz to feminist porn theorist Linda Williams, from psychoanalytic readings to Marxist materialism, it all seemed strangely disconnected from my direct experience of cinema. This reflects, more than anything, the formative effect of my early readings on cinema: those teenage days spent in the aisles of the local library, surreptitiously ripping out porno images from *Stargazer*[18] (a book on the early films of Andy Warhol) or reading the harsh writing of Pauline Kael and James Agee. This Yankee toughness—which, paradoxically, I despised in the real world of international politics—was the kind of writing I was attracted to. No-one could accuse Kael or Agee of being self-delusional when it came to film—limited by their prejudices, sure. An annoying unshakeable faith in the tenets of liberalism can still piss me off, though.

These two critics more than any others managed to hone my own critical faculties, even if only so I could carry on internal disagreements with their own evaluations. Surfing the crest of first love, losing my cherry to the enormous world of movies yet undiscovered, I could not quite understand their easy dismissal of so many films, so many talents. So I had to construct intricate arguments in order to deflate what I saw as their wilful blindness.

Years later, I can see that Kael was right about so much that I thought she was wrong about back then. Bob Fosse's *All That Jazz*, for example, is indeed a series of impressive set pieces disappearing up its own incoherent arsehole. When I first saw it on its release in 1979, when I did not know about Fellini's *8½*, when fractured narrative was something I had never come across, I went back to see Fosse's movie again and again. I almost hated Kael when I came across her withering review of it.[19] It's only with hindsight that I realised, having seen the Fellini movie, that she was right in some of her acid comments. I also realise that nothing can change my love for that film. It's not just a film I saw back in 1979. It is also a mood, a certain memory, a certain time.

In 1990, doing my backpacker thing across Europe and the States, I took a subway from my aunt's place in Queens and went into Manhattan. I went into the *New Yorker* building and took the lift to the magazine's offices. 'I'd like to see Ms. Pauline Kael', I squealed nervously, sweating with anxiety, 'I know she must be busy, but I've come all the way from Australia'. The man at the desk looked at me with a combination of dismissive arrogance and tender mocking. 'The lady works from home.' It was one of those moments when I realise again I'm just a small town boy: a Waite in the woodshed.

Nostalgia is, I believe, one of the things to watch out for when it comes to criticism. That's why the severe stripped-back language of American criticism allows for a constant monitoring of the seemingly instinctual tendency in criticism to romanticise the past —whether it's Norman Mailer describing a fight, Mark Twain mocking the solemnities of Europe, Camille Paglia deflating feminist mythologising and patriarchal ostentation or James Agee piercing Hollywood sentimentality. This toughness, this insistence on intellectual lucidity and poetic sparseness, also allows for going out on a limb, staking the grand critical claim. I'm not referring to a *Who Weekly* rating system here, or the kind of gushing reviews which claim a cinematic masterpiece every few weeks: if only that was the case. Being tough means being exacting and sometimes harsh, and all the writers above have a whiplash satiric tone that hurts.

Being tough can also mean standing by your passions. Pauline Kael was mocked for comparing the New York opening of Bertolucci's *Last Tango in Paris* to the first scandalous performance of Stravinsky's *Rites of Spring* in Paris. Agee's fascinating, perplexed and righteous review of Chaplin's *Monsieur Verdoux* states a claim for greatness which has as much to do with Chaplin's disgraceful treatment by the McCarthyists as it has to do with the movie itself. Ultimately the question of whether they were wrong or right in their judgments needs to be put up against a plethora of contemporary theoretical writings on film which can span hundreds of pages and give you no damn idea what the author thought of a single film. You have to *assume* that passion motivates these contemporary writers' decisions to write on their chosen films or genre. That's an assumption that's deadening when it comes to writing passionate critical commentary.[20]

Opinion in criticism isn't enough. Certain critical theoretical models and movements have been crucial for making me understand not only my relationship to individual films and narratives, but also assisting me to understand the economic and social contexts of the production, distribution and reproduction of film. The critical literature of the United States assumes a straightforward democratic egalitarianism counterposed to European stuffy aristocracy. The truth is: the crucial relevance of working-class experience in my coming to an understanding of the world—crucial in the sense that it was never simply academic for me but real, lived, constant and something that won't go away—is not something that Americans seem adequate at understanding. (It's possible, however, that if I had been born black *and* working class I might find reassuring support in a US writer such as bell hooks and a filmmaker such as Charles Burnett.) Queer independent cinema in the United States, the interrogative Marxist (and post-Marxist) cinema of Godard, Rainer Werner Fassbinder and Pier Paolo Pasolini, and the great humanist works of Russian, Scandinavian, Iranian and Japanese cinema— all these have been dense and emotional encounters with film which have formed part of a dialogue in which I've tried to address questions of ethics and economy, sexuality and responsibility, theology and existential adriftness.

So when I make the claim that *I don't get film theory*, I am not saying I don't read film theory or even that I may not necessarily understand film theory. I just don't believe that the experience of cinema can be distilled to a pure model of effect and affect. It's too mongrel an art for that. When I did come to finally crack the auteur theory, I realised I couldn't bring myself to have faith in it. I liked it too much when directors broke through their own styles and conventions. And it's always struck me that the editor, the performer, the cinematographer and the scriptwriter have as much to do with the pleasures of movie going as does the director. And beyond personalities, film is not only art but it is also commerce and technology; it is in history and part of politics.

I guess I'm saying that film is not enough. The first thing I do straight after a film festival these days is head back to a public library and immerse myself in reading and words: history and science and philosophy, rarely fiction. Knowing cinema a little, as I think I do, I've realised it's actually very rare when an image is equal to a thousand words.

A small-town boy falls in love with a film at thirteen. I fell in love with the fall of light on bodies and water, but I also fell in love with a film about boyhood that spoke to me with an Australian accent. I've suggested how things like class, nationality and sexuality can effect how we perceive a film, and how understanding something of the historical context of a society—Autumn, 1953—can allow for re-interpretations and the exploration of themes left silent or half-spoken. Of course, you've got to watch that nostalgia doesn't bind you to obstinate assertions; but I think that when it comes to something like understanding our engagement with film, we will always be bound somewhat by our age and context.

By age, I mean very simply, that as no-one can escape being *in* history, some things as basic as your age, your maturity, the date when you saw a film will make all the difference to an aesthetic response. I saw *Last Tango in Paris* at eighteen and snickered all the way through. I saw it again ten years later and I cried my broken heart out.

By place, I mean very simply, that we are still in nations and still in language. Maybe I feel this acutely being an Australian, which means being *of* the west but not *in* the west, and particularly being an Australian for whom English was not a first language. We need our national cinema so we don't forget how and where we live, how we speak: Schepisi, Moffatt, John Hillcoat in *Ghosts...of the Civil Dead*, Clara Law in *A Floating Life*, and more recently Ivan Sen in *Tears* and *Dust,* and Cate Shortland in *Joy* and *Pentuphouse*. The image can speak with an Australian accent.

I saw *The Devil's Playground* again recently, in a beautifully restored 35 mm print. More than a decade had passed since seeing it again for that second time, on video. My student days were far behind me. I had been working for over half my life. After leaving the cinema, still stirred and overwhelmed by a film that I've carried with me for nearly twenty-five years, I went to have a beer, and listened in to a conversation between two young men who had also seen the film. They were dissing it for its narrative incoherence. *It has no plot, what the fuck happened?* I felt anger then, that unique venomous fury of a film buff, that moment when a matter of taste becomes a matter of principle. I wanted to yell at them, yell something along the lines: *Film isn't just entertainment, you Lara Croft Stepford cocksuckers, there's a space for ellipses, tangents and explorations. Without this space realist cinema would not exist and most of genre cinema would fossilise into a series of vacant repetitive gestures. Is that what you want: cinema to be like a video game?* And then, as if to remind me of the danger of assumptions, the younger one added: *And why should I care about what goes on in a fucking private school?*

I realised, in the brisk chilly air, that I would always have an affection for Tom Allen, but I was one of the men now, one of the Brothers, not one of the boys: working, arguing, resisting, failing and compromising.

I caught the tram back home.

I hope that I've made clear some of the reasons why we should care about what goes on in *The Devil's Playground*. And I hope it also makes sense that given all that, I think the young man outside the cinema was asking quite a good question.

2000

*An undisciplined mind
is the devil's
playground.*
Brother Francine

The shooting of Brother Francine's nightmare: The sirens are dragging him down to Hell.

The first thing I notice is the bright, stark intensity of the title credit panels. The restored cinema print is a revelation after years of seeing the film only in the washed-out, flat tones of video. When the titles end and the first frames of film open to glorious sunlight, and through a boy's eyes we glide up river, I sit back in my seat with a rapturous grin on my face.

The Devil's Playground plays like a fugue in which Tom Allen is the central melody. As the other characters are introduced, their own relationships to faith and to their own bodies illuminate the struggle Tom has to undergo in order to decide for his own or God's will. There is a visual refrain to which we consistently return throughout the film, a melody of montage we will see again and again. Lights are turned on, Tom awakes in a piss-stained bed, we see him washing the sheets in a tub, hanging them out in the courtyard, running through the impressive corridors of the church and breathlessly rushing in late to morning prayers. This melody, which depending on the context of its recurrence in the film, can be either comic or sad, is a perfect summation of Tom's character. He is obedient and dutiful, but also, finally, untameable. This is what makes him the focal point of so much adoration and concern.

The film itself plays out as a series of movements, each one increasingly drawing Tom into a circle from which he will force himself to flee. This fleeing is Tom's liberation because it indicates that his conscious will has finally caught up to the rebelliousness and spirit of his body.

The first movement occurs in the fading light of autumn. The sun's light is still bright and the sky above the seminary is immense. We are introduced to the boys swimming in the lake. Amongst this scene of joyous youthful frivolity, including a friendly tussle between the two young friends, Waite and Allen, there is a reminder of mortality. *The water gets so cold it can freeze you to death.* In the showers, the stern authoritarian Brother Francine storms

Religious instruction: The boys in the chapel.

into the cubicle where Tom is showering in the nude. He delivers a fire-and-brimstone message about the uncleanliness of the body and reminds the boys to 'practice self-denial, self-examination, self-discipline'. We will hear echoes of this very soon when the bookish, theology-obsessed Turner turns this mantra into a masochistic challenge for himself.

In a rapid montage we are shown the boys at their

evening activities: singing around the piano, playing chess, we even see Turner indulging in darning a sock, a slight but telling embellishment for this character who will be increasingly defined by his perversity. (I'm quite prepared to believe that darning socks was an activity all boys had to

Physical instruction: The boys being aroused by lingerie ads.

perform at a boarding school—and therefore not necessarily 'feminine'—but the point is Turner is the only boy we see engaged in this work.) Then the boys prepare for bed and the lights go out. There is a fade.

And fade up to morning. We see the Brothers rising, waking the boys, and we realise that Tom has wet his bed. In the seamlessly edited montage, we see Tom wash his sheets, hang them up to dry, run down the corridor and go late into mass.

The film's second movement begins. We are being introduced to the institution itself. Tom awaits counselling from one of the Brothers and, finding himself alone in a hallway, he takes the opportunity to masturbate over an advertisement for women's lingerie he sees in a magazine. We see the Brothers teaching, and we see them in their common room. They are already articulating the tension between authority and resistance, God and will, that will be the central concern of the film, and which will play out over the very bodies of the men and boys.

While the adults argue, Tom and Waite are in the woodshed, and through half-stutters and giggles, tentatively explore the subject of sex. *You got hair yet?* Their nervous ticks, their tense hands say much more than words about the excruciating changes puberty is wreaking on their bodies and their minds. Inside the common room, Brother Victor watches the schoolyard through the window while the young Brother James plays the piano. It's not natural, Brother Victor says of the clerical life. These two scenes between children and adults mirror each other. The boys are illuminated by a winterish, bright white light. The men are half-immersed in shadow. This is one of many sequences which will see the two Brothers together. They form a couple within the seminary.

We 'see' the melody again. Emerging from a fade out, we are back to endless morning. Once more, Tom has wet the bed, has to wash the sheets and is late for prayers.

The third movement moves us into winter. Tom is seen being influenced by two very different friends. The older boy, Fitz, is handsome, masculine, and we are first introduced to him in a strongly physical role: sawing timber. Tom assists him and we are aware that he hero-worships this older youth. Turner, his thick black glasses always slipping off his face, is Fitz's opposite. Intellectual where Fitz is physical, feminine where Fitz is masculine, Turner's obsession is religion and, in particular, the role of martyrdom in his Catholic faith. Taking Brother Francine's utterings to an extreme, Turner insists to Tom that through 'discipline, concentration and meditation', they will be able to attain a truly religious experience.

The sanctuary of faith: The Brothers in their common room.

Counter to how Tom's relationships with his friends are represented, inside the common room—which throughout the film increasingly appears to be a sanctuary—the Brothers are playing pool and discussing the rights and wrongs of their religious vows.

It is Victor's vehement belief that the school is a 'breeding ground for bloody poofters'. In the midst of this, old Brother Sebastian sits quietly until he breaks into an impassioned ode to masturbation. The Brothers ignore the old man even though his proximity to death confronts the very dilemma they are facing with the inescapable animal and mortal physicality of their flesh.

In answer to Brother Sebastian's cry, we see Tom in near darkness descend into a grotto in which Turner and two other boys are performing sado-masochistic flagellation in an attempt to overcome the carnal body. Tom flees in the darkness while the other boys give chase. He is saved by Fitz. The moonlight becomes visible again. Standing on the jetty of the lake, the two boys discuss the school and their faith. Tom says that he hopes to die in a state of grace. Fitz snorts with laughter and answers, 'You, you'll probably die playing with yourself'. He tells Tom of an expulsion at the school and how all contact with the expelled boy has to end—a premonition of the situation which will finally force Tom to abandon his religious vocation. The scene ends in an abrupt cut which reveals a new morning.

We are into the body of the film now and this central movement removes us from the seminary grounds. The boys go on an excursion. On the bus Turner attempts to convince Tom of the success of the rituals he is performing on his body. (He shows the incredulous Tom a burn scar he received from allowing a flame to eat at his flesh for ten minutes.) Brother Sebastian calls Tom over and warns him to avoid fanatics such as Turner. 'You keep your innocence, Tom … You have a smile that will take you halfway around the world.'

Brothers Victor, James and Francine undertake their own excursion to Melbourne. It is here where Victor and Francine have to deal with the powerful call of their temptations. Francine will be tormented by the flesh he witnesses in a suburban swimming pool; Victor will flirt with two women at a pub. Brother James refuses to drink with the women and goes out to wait in the car. Victor makes his escape, they pick up Francine and a drunk Victor crashes the car on their way back to school. Played as a comic denouement, this car crash jars every time I watch the film. Francine's day at the pool will return in his nightmares of the sirens dragging him down into Hell. We will not witness Brother Victor or Brother James' nightmares. I've come to understand the car crash as a desire for death. Brother Victor is often shown with a glass of whisky in hand. If not death, he is seeking oblivion.

The next day Tom's family arrives to take him away as a treat. This perfect idyll consists of singing and fishing, and there is warmth and generosity in the affection the family members display towards one another. Whatever his battles of faith, familial angst is something young Tom Allen has no need to deal with. His mother informs him that she will stay for a few days in a guesthouse close by. A group of schoolgirls are staying there, as well as a young actor and his accountant friend, who is introduced to Tom. The actor is certainly played as camp, but Tom's attention is firmly on the girls.

Back at school, we hear the melody repeated but this time it sounds insistent, jarring. The cuts from the bed wetting to the sheet washing to the hanging out of the sheets come fast. Tom goes back to the guesthouse. A conversation about vocation between Tom and the actor is interrupted by two young schoolgirls. Tom runs after them. He seems truly gleeful. Chasing one of the girls into a wooded glade, they kiss under autumnal leaves and promise to write to one another. He asks her to write to him as a 'cousin'. He fears that otherwise he would be refused access to her letters. In this movie dominated by the faces of men, there is a luscious soft glint to the skin of Tom's mother and of his 'girlfriend'.

From this point on, the film moves furiously towards its climax. Father Marshall arrives to lead the three day retreat of silence and meditation. Taking confession from the boys, offering advice and a friendly ear to the brothers, he seems free of spiritual angst and anguish. Only Brother Francine seems resentful of the man's good-natured religiosity. On the eve of the retreat Father Marshall delivers a sermon of thunderous, Old Testament terror. The God he invokes is aloof and unforgiving, the only eternal life described is the agony and medieval nightmare of Hell. The smiling face of God is revealed to be another manifestation of the Deity, one which broaches no reconciliation between flesh and soul. The boys and the men enact their retreat, the silence only broken when Tom throws stones into the lake and his act is encouraged by a growing group of rebels.

Increasingly, Tom's patience begins to abandon him. At the end of the retreat he is again denied a celebratory soft drink because of fear that he might wet the bed. When Waite forces another wrestling tussle, Tom allows him to win and then demands that they masturbate each other till they both ejaculate. Waite is ignorant of orgasm. The perplexed young boy's reaction, however, is played for comic effect. In the darkness, however, I perceive something else: an affection and a desire for Tom that Waite has not yet discovered how to articulate, even to himself ... but this is all in my imagining. We will not encounter Waite again.

Tom is forbidden from receiving his 'cousin's' letters; his faith is close to abandonment. A dying Brother Sebastian takes him aside to assure him that a secular life may indeed be a finer calling than that of the priesthood. Tom's crisis of faith is mirrored in the tortured erotic dreams of Brother Francine who breaks down in the common room and declares that contrary to God, 'the body will not be denied'. The young Turner is revealed as missing. Tom remembers the boy boasting that his desire for self-mortification is leading him to the point where he can brave the freezing winter water. In the night, the frozen lake is searched and Turner's body is discovered.

The death of faith: Searching for Turner's body.

In the ensuing scandal, the rules are made stricter, and Tom discovers that Fitz has been asked to leave. Tom cannot learn where the older boy has gone, and he is told that he should now consider his friend as good as dead. A decision is made.

Increasingly in the latter half of the film, the bright greens, reds and yellows of the early autumn have been replaced by the dark blues and cold whites of winter light. But on making his escape, as Brother Victor's car takes him further away from the seminary, the light is again radiant, almost golden. The boy and his body are free.

The film finishes and I wait till the credits are finished. I am one of the few people left in the cinema. I wipe my eyes. I rise to my feet and walk out into the cold Melbourne air.

I am thinking of Waite. I'm imagining a scene that is not in the movie, but surely is implied: that this young boy will ask where his friend has gone, that this young boy will be told that he is to consider Tom Allen as good as dead. Will I imagine that Waite too will run away? Maybe that is one possible scenario but you have to realise that I have been revisiting this film for over twenty years. Over those two decades the characters have been re-imagined in poses and in situations as firmly as if I had seen the scenes enacted out on celluloid.

These are the scenes in my head ... I allow Brother Francine moments of happiness in meditation and grace. I replace his nightmares with dreams in which he is comforted by angels. I want to give him a complexity that is not his due in the film. I have Brother Victor fight a tougher battle. The nymphs that drag him down into the silent water have the bodies and the youthful flesh of the boys he teaches. He fondles, he touches, he breaks his vows and he betrays trust. I have Brother James hold him, comfort him, all the while refusing to betray his own vows of celibacy—but the anguish in the desire is of such intensity that in holding him, the younger man comes. I am enacting my revenge for the film's squeamish terror of sexual perversity. And does Waite run away? I've made him a working-class wog boy, remember. He argues against the Movement, he hides a picture of Lenin in his Bible, he learns the pleasure of tussling with the bourgeois boys, conquering them and getting them to blow him off. Where would a working-class fag like Waite go? He should stay, of course. Play it safe, of course. Obviously I make him a hero, like Tom, on the road. He makes good his escape, but first he gets to fuck Nick Tate.

The stories in my head are not in the film; they are there because the film cannot age with me and so I age with it. But I'm more than happy with the memories themselves: of Simon Burke's smile that takes you halfway around the world; of the sun skipping across water and falling on bluestone; the solid glowing flesh of boys and girls, of women and men; the insistent rain falling on the school's quadrangle; a boy rubbing his cold and nervous hands; and the golden light of afternoon in the twilight of an Antipodean summer.

NOTES

1 Pauline Kael, *For Keeps* (Plume, 1996, pp 913–915).

2 *The Seventh Seal*, which is an evocation of Bergman's adult loss of faith, uses the medieval landscape of the Black Plague as a representation of what a godless world would be like. The film's famous scenes of Death playing chess with the Knight are certainly unforgettable and one of cinema's most vivid images— but what most terrified me as an adolescent were the scenes of the marching procession of penitents, whipping and scarring themselves, and of the young girl about to be burnt as a witch. The power in these scenes lies precisely in their suggestion that whether the world is with or without God, life is suffering and evil is unavoidable. Godlessness is innocence in *The Devil's Playground*, free from terror, and I suspect that this is one of the reasons Kael attributed 'paganism' to Schepisi's film.

3 Frank Hardy, *Power Without Glory* (1950).

4 John Williams, of course, is most famous for his scores for blockbuster movies like *Jaws* and *Star Wars*. Bill Conti scored *Rocky*, a theme that was a soundtrack to my childhood.

5 Tom Keneally's novel, *The Chant of Jimmie Blacksmith* (1972), was influenced by Frank Clune's book about the life of the Aboriginal bushranger, *Jimmy Governor* (1959). Born in 1875, Governor married Ethel Page, a 16-year-old white woman, in 1898 and was executed in 1901.

6 *Ben Hall* was an ABC/BBC co-production about a nineteenth-century Australian bushranger. *Against the Wind* was a commercial mini-series about the Australian convict past.

7 In his remarkable short film, *Dust*, Ivan Sen indicates that the terror that lies hidden beneath the desert landscape is precisely history itself, and most particularly the 'hidden' history of war and massacre against indigenous Australians. The most well-known Australian film to deal with this terror of the land is Peter Weir's *Picnic at Hanging Rock*, a film in which Aborigines are absent. Is it possible to address the mystery of the disappearance of the girls from Hanging Rock by addressing this absence? The exemplary film about the horror of the outback remains *Wake in Fright* which, without directly dealing with the dispossession of the outback, grounds the terror in European savagery and violence.

8   For an eclectic read through the traumas of being a music fan, I recommend *Love is the Drug*, edited by John Aizlewood (Penguin, 1994). For a spot-on filmic representation of the fan and our (queer) relationship to pop culture, you can't beat *Velvet Goldmine*.

9   *Reds* is about US political journalist, John Reed, who went to the USSR in 1917 and wrote about the Bolshevik revolution in *Ten Days That Shook The World* (1919).

10 J. D. Salinger, *The Catcher in the Rye* (1951); Brett Easton Ellis, *Less Than Zero* (1985); Emily Bronte, *Wuthering Heights* (1847).

11 I am using the term 'Movie Brats' as a general term for the film-school educated US directors who came to prominence in the early 1970s; see Linda Myles and Michael Pye's book of the same name (Holt Reinhart & Wilson, 1979). Even more influential for me— as they essayed and gave voice to 'counter-cultural' and/or radical politics and aesthetics— were filmmakers such as Robert Altman, Hal Ashby and Haskell Wexler who are not necessarily of the film- school 'Brat' group but who worked alongside them. (One of the most astonishing adolescent nights of my life was not being able to sleep and seeing Wexler's *Medium Cool* on late night TV. *Medium Cool* combines a fictional narrative about a television cameraman (Robert Forster) with cinéma-vérité documentary sequences set during the 1968 Democrat Convention in Chicago, which resulted in a riot in which students were gunned down by the military. Try going back to high school after that experience!)

12 There is also an ambiguous encounter Tom has at the guesthouse where his parents are staying, in which he meets a camp actor and his accountant 'friend'. The actor, certainly, is coded as 'gay'. This 'coding' escaped me as a youth but was very obvious when I returned to the film. After a conversation with these two men, Tom chases a schoolgirl and has his first heterosexual experience. It is difficult not to read this sequence of events as anything other than an attempt to verify Tom's 'natural' heterosexuality.

13 Santamaria was, however, a child of Italian immigrants and his parents ran a fruit shop in the then Melbourne working-class suburb of Brunswick. If I had known that back then it might have tempered my dislike for him—but, again, I just might have thought of him as

something worse: a class traitor.

14 Unlike the Western Church, the Orthodox Church (that is, an Eastern Church) did not present an image of Christ as vulnerable and meek as is widespread through most of Catholic and Protestant iconography. I feared Christ growing up and it was to his mother, Mary, that I looked to for sympathy in my prayers. This difference between the churches underlines an ability to view *The Devil's Playground* with a sometimes detached 'pagan' eye and sometimes to respond immediately and emotionally to the religious traumas of the boys and brothers.

15 *Right...Said Fred: Fred Schepisi, Director*, directed by Don Featherstone (Don Feathersone Productions/SBS TV, 1993).

16 It is interesting that while Turner wants to involve Tom in the rites and fundamentalism of Catholic mysticism, the actor Tom meets at the guesthouse interrogates him about the meaning of his Catholic faith. In both instances, Tom seems uninterested in intellectual questions about his beliefs. In terms of Australian cultural practice, this further accentuates the 'naturalness' of his sexuality as opposed to the 'intellectualism' of the deviant characters.

17 Australian films in the 1970s did not, however, have the intellectual rigour of contemporaneous European cinema. For example, there is nothing comparable in these films to the subverting and confronting of Hollywood convention and genre by the new German cinema.

18 Stephen Koch, *Stargazer* (1973).

19 Nevertheless, I still love *All That Jazz*, love it despite its self-importance, love it for its indulgence. The point is that Kael's criticism in the *New Yorker* led me to argument and to critical awareness—but I still don't think she was right all the time.

20 I have deliberately chosen not to refer to a particular text. There are many I could have chosen as examples, but I didn't feel like being a bitch about it. These solemn tomes have a limited readership, and as there are enough right-wingers at the moment only too happy to kick academics, I want to be careful not to align myself with them. Let's just say that apposite to this dry theoretical tendency in modern film writing, Jonathan Rosenbaum's writings stand out as a clear and refreshing antidote. I'd call him tough, as well.

BIBLIOGRAPHY

Agee, James. *Agee on Film: Criticism and Comment on the Movies.* New York: Modern Library, 2000.

Kael, Pauline. *For Keeps.* New York City: Plume, 1996.

McKinlay, Brian. *A Documentary History of the Australian Labor Movement 1850–1975.* Richmond, Australia: Drummond, 1979.

McMullin, Ross. *The Light on the Hill: The Australian Labor Party, 1891–1991.* Melbourne: Oxford University Press, 1991.

Mailer, Norman. *The Time of Our Time.* New York: Modern Library, 1998.

Mathews, Sue. *35 mm Dreams: Conversations With Five Directors About the Australian Film Revival.* Ringwood, Victoria: Penguin, 1984.

Paglia, Camille. *Sexual Personae: Art and Decadence from Nefertiti to Emily Dickinson.* New York: Vintage, 1990.

Penguin Macquarie Dictionary of Australian Politics. Ringwood, Victoria: Penguin Australia, 1988.

Rosenbaum, Jonathan. *Movies as Politics.* Berkley, California: University of California Press, 1997.

Brother James (Peter Cox):
Between boyhood and adulthood.

Rushdie, Salman. *The Wizard of Oz: An Appreciation.* London: British Film Institute, 1997.

Stratton, David. *The Avacado Plantation: Boom and Bust in the Australian Film Industry.* Chippendale, NSW: Pan McMillan, 1990.

Uren, Tom. *Straight Left.* Milsons Point, NSW: Random House Australia, 1994.

Wood, Robin. *Hollywood: From Vietnam to Reagan.* New York: Columbia University Press, 1986.

FILMOGRAPHY

Against the Wind (TV series), Simon Wincer, 1978

Alien, Ridley Scott, 1979

All That Jazz, Bob Fosse, 1979

BeDevil, Tracey Moffatt, 1993

Ben Hall (TV series), Frank Charles Arnold, Don Chaffey & Peter Maxwell, 1975

Breaker Morant, Bruce Beresford, 1980

Carnal Knowledge, Mike Nichols, 1971

The Chant of Jimmie Blacksmith, Fred Schepisi, 1977

Coming Home, Hal Ashby, 1978

Don's Party, Bruce Beresford, 1976

Dust, Ivan Sen, 2000

8½, Federico Fellini, 1963

Evil Angels (USA and UK: *A Cry in the Dark*), Fred Schepisi, 1988

A Floating Life, Clara Law, 1996

Gallipoli, Peter Weir, 1981

The Getting of Wisdom, Bruce Beresford, 1977

Ghosts…of the Civil Dead, John Hillcoat, 1989

The Gleaners and I/Les Glaneurs et la Glaneuse, Agnes Varda, 2001

Gone With the Wind, Victor Fleming, George Cukor & Sam Wood, 1939

The Graduate, Mike Nichols, 1967

Greetings From Wollongong, Mary Callaghan, 1982

The Illustrated Auschwitz, Jackie Farkas, 1992

It Happened One Night, Frank Capra, 1934

Jaws, Steven Spielberg, 1975

Journey Among Women, Tom Cowan, 1977

Joy, Cate Shortland, 2001

Kes, Ken Loach, 1969

Klute, Alan J. Pakula, 1971

Lacombe, Lucien, Louis Malle, 1975

Last Tango in Paris, Bernardo Bertolucci, 1972

The Last Wave, Peter Weir, 1977

Lost in the Bush, Peter Dodds, 1973

The Man From Snowy River, George Miller, 1982

Medium Cool, Haskell Wexler, 1969

Midnight Cowboy, John Schlesinger, 1969

Monsieur Verdoux, Charles Chaplin, 1942

Murmur of the Heart/Souffle au Coeur, Louis Malle, 1971

1900, Bernardo Bertolucci, 1976

Padre Padrone, Paolo Taviani & Vittorio Taviani, 1977

Pentuphouse, Cate Shortland, 2001

Picnic at Hanging Rock, Peter Weir, 1975

Reds, Warren Beatty, 1981

The Right Stuff, Philip Kaufman, 1983

Rocky, John G. Avildsen, 1976

The Seventh Seal, Ingmar Bergman, 1957

Shoah, Claude Lanzmann, 1985

Star Wars, George Lucas, 1977

Tears, Ivan Sen, 1998

The Tree of Wooden Clogs, Ermanno Olmi, 1978

Preparing the actors for 1953: Fred Schepisi, centre.

An Unmarried Woman, Paul Mazursky, 1978

Until the End of the World, Wim Wenders, 1991

Velvet Goldmine, Todd Haynes, 1998

Wake in Fright, Ted Kotcheff, 1971

Weekend, Jean-Luc Godard, 1968

Where the Green Ants Dream, Werner Herzog, 1984

Winter of Our Dreams, John Duigan, 1981

The Year My Voice Broke, John Duigan, 1987

CREDITS

Production/release year
1976

Production company
Feature Film House

KEY CREW

Director
Fred Schepisi

Producer
Fred Schepisi

Production manager
Greg Tepper

Assistant director
Mal Bryning

Assistant director
Rhonda Schepisi

Script
Fred Schepisi

Cinematography
Ian Baker

Editor
Brian Kavanagh

Art director
Trevor Ling

Costumes
Bruce Finlayson

Make-up
Anne Pospischil

Title design
Al Et Al

Music
Bruce Smeaton

Sound recording
Don Connolly

Sound re-recording
Peter Fenton

Sound re-recording
United Sound

Sound editor
Edward
McQueen-Mason

Running time
107

Colour system
Eastmancolor

KEY CAST

Arthur Dignam
Brother Francine

Nick Tate
Brother Victor

Simon Burke
Tom Allen

Charles McCallum
Brother Sebastian

John Frawley
Brother Celian

Jonathan Hardy
Brother Arnold

Gerry Duggan
Father Hanrahan

Peter Cox
Brother James

John Diedrich
Fitz

Tom Keneally
Father Marshall

Sheila Florance
Mrs. Sullivan

Ann Phelan
Jillian Archer
Girls in pub

Gerda Nicolson
Mrs. Allen

John Proper
Mr. Allen

Bill Kelly
Farmer

Vicki Bray
Miss Weatherhead

Hannah Govan
Miss Doyle

Danee Lindsay
Lynette

Michael Carman
Nigel Ryan

Iain Murton
Brian Anderson

Alan Cinis
Waite

Warren Coleman
Westaway

Gary Pixton
Tomkin

Richard Morgan
Smith

Rowan Currie
Casey

Director and cinemtographer: Fred Schepisi and Ian Baker.

Wayne Comley
Mahoney

Michael David
Turner

Marc Gough
Brown

Andrew Court
Woolmore

Brett Murphy
Tierman

Deborah Schepisi
Janine Schepisi
Quentin Schepisi
Jason Schepisi
Allen children